Shma Koleinu

A Jewish People's Commentary on the Siddur

Rabbi Steven A. Schwarzman

Shma Koleinu: A Jewish People's Commentary on the Siddur

ISBN-13 978-1505353921
ISBN: 1505353920

First Edition.

Hebrew Siddur selections taken from DavkaWriter Hebrew-English word processor text library, © Davka Corporation, www.davka.com. Used with permission.

Grateful acknowledgement is given to the Jewish Theological Seminary of America for permission to republish the selections by Rabbi Samuel Barth.

Grateful acknowledgement is given to Frances Kraft for permission to include selections from a book she is writing about the year she lost her father.

Grateful acknowledgement is given to Rabbi Jack H Bloom, Ph.D., for permission to include selections from his book, *The Rabbi as Symbolic Exemplar: By the Power Vested in Me.*

Cover art © Rafael Ben-Ari / Dollar Photo Club.

For my parents, who taught me,
for Bettina, who learns with me,
and for our children, who now learn on their own

Contents

Barukh She'amar

Shma

V'ahavta

V'ahavta

Chapter 5   Amidah

Amidah or Shemoneh Esrai?

Mehayeh Hameitim

Atah Kadosh

Kedushah

Hashiveinu

Selah Lanu

Refa'enu

Refa'enu

Chapter 1
Introduction

The prayers of "ordinary" people turn out to be powerful, focused, deep, and poignant. Who knew?

In the modern world, many of us have lost the ability to pray. Or we think we have. But there are ordinary people out there, just like us, who have found particular prayers that speak to them eloquently and personally.

And when prayers speak to us, we can speak through those prayers to God.

Shma Koleinu – Hear Our Voice – is itself a prayer in the *siddur* (the Jewish prayerbook). We pray for God to hear our voice, and we pray for the ability to find our voice.

– Rabbi Steven A. Schwarzman

The Power of "Ordinary" People's Prayers

Rabbi Steven A. Schwarzman

It can be a strange task sometimes, serving as a rabbi in a congregation. Much of my work life, or at least the most publicly visible part of that work life, centers around public prayer at the synagogue.

People need prayers to be familiar, because in that familiarity comes comfort, both on a day-to-day or week-to-week basis, and especially during times of spiritual crisis.

And people need prayers to be inspiring, a quality that is sometimes in tension with the quality of familiarity. The problem is not new: in the Talmud's tractate Berakhot, almost two millennia ago, the rabbis discussed the dangers of letting one's prayers become rote.

So as a rabbi, I want prayer to be meaningful for the members of my congregation. And at the same time, since I am called to "officiate" at services, I am also responsible for making sure they end reasonably on time. Not very conducive to meaningful prayer, perhaps, but a necessary part of life.

While there is a definite trend to lower the height of the *bimah* in many synagogues, and in general to make prayer a closer, more immanent experience, this, too, is a learning process for all involved, including rabbis. And so it came as a surprise to me one day, when I decided to ask people to name their favorite prayer, that I got an amazing response.

It was early in a Saturday morning service. We were short of a *minyan*, a quorum of 10 adults, and so we needed to stall for a few minutes until more people arrived. The people who are there at the beginning of the service are usually comfortable with the *siddur*, the Jewish prayer book. They've been reading these prayers and indeed these very pages all their lives; in many cases, without having been taught much about what the words mean, but reading and voicing them nonetheless as an act of very pure devotion.

And when I asked this group to name their favorite prayers, I honestly wasn't expecting much. I thought, uncharitably, that perhaps they had never given the subject much thought.

And I was completely wrong.

In that small group of early-morning *daveners*, one after the other in my congregation at the time, Beth Israel in Bangor, Maine, easily and movingly articulated what his or her favorite prayer was, and why.

For one, it was *Shma*. Every time he said it, it made him reflect on the oneness of God. Wow! Every time! I wish that every time I prayed a prayer, I could focus like that on the meaning of the words.

One by one, they all mentioned their own favorites, and you will read some of their thoughts in this book. After half a dozen people, without so much as having to turn a page to find the prayer they were referencing, spoke about their favorite prayers in the Jewish liturgy, I began to realize that we were on to something.

And I realized also that the only reason that I didn't *know* how deeply these people were praying on a regular basis was because I had never thought to ask.

Traditional Jewish prayer, as you will find it in Orthodox and most Conservative synagogues, is usually done entirely in Hebrew, with perhaps a few English readings here and there – most often the prayer for the country, which is itself based on an ancient tradition of praying for the welfare of the land where one resides and for wisdom to be given to its rulers.

Traditional Jewish prayer is incredibly rich and deep. But it has what they call in the business world relatively high entry barriers. You have to know at least some Hebrew, even if you are actually praying in translation, in order to know where the congregation is in the service. The concepts are, in many cases, very ancient ones, and sometimes people are challenged to connect to ideas from another time, even if what they express is timeless. And, over the centuries, the core of the Jewish prayer service has been richly and beautifully supplemented with many prayers of introduction, of warm-ups, of inspiration, of liturgical poems, and more – which means that the Sabbath morning prayer service now takes three hours for many congregations. That is a high entry barrier, indeed.

And yet, here were the members of my own congregation very movingly showing how seriously they take Jewish prayer. It may have looked like rote mumbling to an outsider, but that was not the deeper reality. These people – "ordinary" only in the sense that they did not have advanced degrees in Jewish studies, though they were all extraordinarily warm and good people – showed me that ordinary Jews can not only have deep insights into the prayers that we say, but that allowing them to share those insights might help other, equally "ordinary" Jews to feel empowered in deepening their own Jewish prayer lives.

Some of the reflections in this book focus on the words or the meaning of a prayer. Others tell the authors' stories, deeply personal stories, of where a prayer takes them. One of these stories is so very personal that the author has asked to remain incompletely identified, a request that I have of course granted.

I have found these stories of "ordinary" people and the prayers that speak to them to be incredibly moving, and I believe you will, too.

A word on usage: just as being on the same page as the rest of the congregation is highly overrated, so, too, is consistency in a book by many authors. If there is a good reason to force writers familiar with Ashkenazi pronunciation to sound unrecognizably (to them) Sephardi, I can't see it. Even more, it would be unfair to change writers' theologies by corralling them into a consistency of language involving God, so I do not do this except for standardizing on "God" instead of "G-d," because not all readers will understand who the latter is, and in any case it is no desecration of God's name to write out "God" in English. (Whatever the *kohen gadol* – the high priest – pronounced in the Temple on Yom Kippur in ancient Jerusalem, it was in Hebrew, not English, so I think we are safe on that score.) Similarly, it would be wrong to homogenize the various usages you will find in the pages that follow, including different translations of the same texts, some more traditional, some more modern, because the writers are of course relating to the texts as *they* use them, not as someone else might. For some writers, pronouns relating to God are capitalized, and for others, not. Hebrew doesn't know from capital letters, so there is room to allow different authors to choose in English.

I thank each of the contributors for sharing their voices. May you be as moved by these reflections as I am, and may their courage in prayer be an inspiration for you, so that your voice, too, can be both sounded and heard.

Chapter 2
Preliminary Blessings

Jewish prayer begins every single day of the year even before we get out of bed. From the moment we wake up, when we say *Modeh* (for men) *or Modah* (for women) *ani lefanekha...* we begin preparing ourselves for another day of life and warming ourselves up for prayer.

– *Rabbi Steven A. Schwarzman*

Modeh/Modah Ani

Mark Wallach

מוֹדֶה/מוֹדָה אֲנִי לְפָנֶיךָ, מֶלֶךְ חַי וְקַיָּם, שֶׁהֶחֱזַרְתָּ בִּי נִשְׁמָתִי בְּחֶמְלָה רַבָּה אֱמוּנָתֶךָ.

The prayer that resonates with me is that which I utter first thing in the morning, *Modeh Ani*. It reminds me that each day is truly a gift. This puts life into perspective and hopefully motivates me to live each day properly and hopefully make a difference even in some small way.

Modeh/Modah Ani

Rabbi Rachel Barenblat

I admit, it's not always my very first thought upon waking. In the early months of parenthood, when I woke many times a night to the sound of the baby's cry, I had a hard time mustering any response beyond exhaustion. But these days I usually wake to the quiet sounds of my toddler babbling. The sweetness of that morning song makes it easier for me to move right into *modah ani l'fanekha, melekh hai v'kayam*.

Most mornings I murmur the *Modah Ani* as I shuffle to the bathroom, pull on my robe, and go downstairs to pour some milk for my little one. Sometimes I sing it to him as we cuddle at the beginning of the day. On other days I don't get to *Modah Ani* until I'm in the shower; I sing it with a sea-chanty tune as the hot falling water soothes my skin and wakes my spirit.

Modah Ani is the prayer for gratitude, meant to be recited first thing upon waking in the morning. ("*Modah*" is the feminine form of the first word, "Grateful;" men recite "*Modeh ani*" instead.) Here's the prayer's text in full:

מודה אני לפניך מלך חי וקים שהחזרת בי נשמתי בחמלה, רבה אמונתך.

Modah ani l'fanekha, melekh hai v'kayam, shehehezarta bi nishmati b'hemlah, rabbah emunatekha! - I am grateful before You, living and enduring God, that You have mercifully restored my soul to me. Great is Your faithfulness!"

It's a simple prayer, but reciting it regularly has changed my life. Almost ten years ago, at a Jewish retreat center in the Catskills, I attended a contemplative morning service led by Rabbi Jeff Roth. He taught us a simple chant, just the first two words of this prayer, repeated again and again. He told us that he wanted us to focus on gratitude while we were singing these words...and if we couldn't access gratitude in that moment, then we might choose to focus on praying that someday we might be able to feel grateful again. I've returned to that teaching more times than I can count.

The *Modah Ani* reminds me that I want to begin each day with thankfulness. I want to meet each day's challenges not with anxiety or resentment, but with gratitude, plain and simple. I'm lucky to be right here, right now. I'm lucky to be alive. God has kept watch over my soul while I slept and has restored it to me this very day so that I might experience whatever comes my way. It's honestly awesome.

Reciting *Modah Ani* helps me connect with my sense of awe. And on days when awe and gratitude seem inaccessibly far away (because let's face it: we all have days like those), I can recite *Modah Ani* with hope that I might be able to get in touch with gratitude again, speedily and soon.

I love the fact that Jewish tradition has given me a prayer for waking up, a mindfulness practice designed to help me begin the day in the way I want to continue: with gratitude in my heart and a blessing on my lips.

Asher Yatzar

Bettina Schwarzman

בָּרוּךְ אַתָּה יְיָ אֱלֹהֵינוּ מֶלֶךְ הָעוֹלָם, אֲשֶׁר יָצַר אֶת הָאָדָם בְּחָכְמָה,
וּבָרָא בוֹ נְקָבִים נְקָבִים, חֲלוּלִים חֲלוּלִים, גָּלוּי וְיָדוּעַ לִפְנֵי כִסֵּא כְבוֹדֶךָ
שֶׁאִם יִפָּתֵחַ אֶחָד מֵהֶם, אוֹ יִסָּתֵם אֶחָד מֵהֶם, אִי אֶפְשָׁר לְהִתְקַיֵּים
וְלַעֲמוֹד לְפָנֶיךָ: בָּרוּךְ אַתָּה יְיָ, רוֹפֵא כָל בָּשָׂר, וּמַפְלִיא לַעֲשׂוֹת:

Asher yatzar et ha'adam behokhma: Every time I study
human anatomy, I am amazed at how intricately and
intelligently our bodies are formed. Could a human
being even begin to think up all the different
functions our bodies perform, and how they
interconnect?

Uvara vo nekavim nekavim halulim halulim - this must
mean the arteries and veins for transporting the
blood, as well as the various passages that form the
digestive and respiratory systems.

*Galui veyadua she'im yipateah ehad mehem o yisatem ehad
mehem, i efshar la'amod ulehitkayem lifnei kisei khevodekha*
– should any of these passages remain open or closed,
we become sick, or even die. If the vascular system
doesn't work, we may have a heart attack. Everyone
knows that if we can't inhale, or exhale, we die within
a few minutes. A failure in the digestive system
doesn't produce effects that are as immediate, but
they are nevertheless equally pernicious. Even before
it gets that serious, enough discomfort results that we
cannot "stand before Your throne of glory." This is
the blessing one should say after going to the
bathroom. This would produce giggles in childhood.

We couldn't understand why something so trivial needed a blessing. However, anyone who has had problems with either urinary tract infections or constipation fully understands the importance of healthy functioning. *Galui veyadua* – it is well known. If these things don't work, we aren't healthy, cannot go about our business, and certainly aren't in a position, or mood, to praise God.

Lifnei kisei khevodekha – before Your throne of glory. We do not live just in order to live, but in order to stand before God's throne of glory. Perhaps this is even a hint to God to make sure we remain able-bodied so that we can serve Him. As the psalmist says: "The dead don't praise God." We are also appealing to God's self-interest here.

The blessing ends with *rofeh kol basar umafli la'asot. He Who heals all flesh.* So is it appropriate to say this blessing whenever one recovers, or wishes to recover from an illness? I heard of a woman who had to have an amputation. More than she worried about losing the limb, she worried about the stump healing. Her rabbi told her to say this berakhah, and doing so gave her some comfort.

The word *mafli* is related to the word *pele*, wondrous, amazing. It is indeed amazing!

Asher Yatzar

Judy Petsonk

What I love about Judaism is its deep appreciation of the everyday miracles of ordinary life. My favorite prayer is the *Asher Yatzar*, which I say every morning during that most humble of activities, sitting on the pot. It is a nice long blessing, giving one ample time to become aware of the complexity and beauty of the delicately balanced inner symphony which is the body. All those tubes and ducts! If I were responsible for having to open and close each one, I'd never get to work. But it all happens without my will or even my attention. How important not to take it all for granted!

At 66, having lived through the prolonged aging and deaths of my parents, I'm very aware that the smooth functioning of all those tubes and ducts, and the health that goes with it, is a limited-time-only gift. I need to give thanks now, while I can, to focus not on the future, not even on this afternoon, but on the miracle of this moment. In the face of that awareness of mortality, the blessing reminds me of three sources of comfort.

First, all life seems to be a closed system. All the food I eat, in a less urbanized world, would become fertilizer for plants which would in turn become food for other animals and humans. I, too, will return to the earth, but I realize that nothing is lost, neither the organic chemicals of living creatures, nor the energy which animates our souls.

Second, there are all kinds of miracles – healing of body and healing of spirit. As one kind of health declines, I can embrace the opportunities to learn wisdom and make peace, with those I love and with myself.

Third is the matter of thrones. I don't tend to think of God as sitting on a throne, or in fact of having a body. Yet in this prayer, I, sitting on my throne, am addressing God sitting on God's throne. Chuckling over the parallel, I realize that even at my most vulnerable, my most ridiculous, my most embarrassing, I am always in the image of God. And so are we all. It's what's at the core that counts.

Asher Yatzar

Erica S. Goldman-Brodie

"You have cancer," Dr. Jean Chin said calmly over the phone after the results of the biopsy came back.

"Clear cell endometrial carcinoma."

My heart sank. First, I would need a hysterectomy to determine the extent of the cancer. As soon as the hysterectomy was over, the surgeon told us the grim news: the cancer had metastasized and the treatment needed to be aggressive if I wanted to beat it.

We, my husband, Joe and I, consulted many doctors and friends who were experts in the field of gynecological oncology, sending slide samples to Harvard and Memorial Sloan Kettering. With a five percent chance of survival, we didn't want to leave any stones unturned. Yes, five percent. I turned to Joe and declared, "There have been people in the five percent, and I'm going to be one of them."

Together, we decided to go the "aggressive" rather than the "wait-and-see-and-hope-for-the-best" route. There was a lot of waiting. The hysterectomy was followed by six weeks of waiting (for the surgical scars to heal), followed by six weeks of radiation and weekly cisplatin chemo, then another six weeks of waiting for the burn marks of the radiation to heal, and the combination chemo of the dreaded carboplatin-taxol where one feels sick, really sick, the hair falls out, and the "chemo mush brain" effect as my friend, Claire has called it, takes over.

During this time, my husband was an amazing source of support. I grew up in Australia. Friends from Australia flew in to spend time with me. My family, friends and community were just wonderfully creative in demonstrating their care and offering much appreciated help.

Having chemo administered is not fun. It's a long process full of delays and waiting. First the nurses hydrate the patient. Then an antihistamine and a steroid to fortify are administered. And then the chemo itself (carboplatin, and the dreaded, hair-falling-out taxol) is administered intravenously by a slow drip.

The Benadryl does make the patient tired, but not less anxious. Friends (and of course my husband) took turns accompanying me to these sessions. For the first session of taxol, the potential side effects and reactions were recited by the staff. In fear, I felt my throat and my stomach restrict simultaneously.

As I watched the taxol enter my vein, I closed my eyes and prayed, prayed hard using my own words. I so regretted not remembering all the words to the *Asher Yatzar* prayer, the prayer recited upon leaving the lavatory.

> *Blessed are You, Hashem our God, King of the universe, Who formed man with wisdom and created within him many openings and many hollows. It is obvious and known before Your*

Throne of Glory that if even one of them ruptures, or if even one of them becomes blocked, it would be impossible to survive and to stand before You (even for a short period). Blessed are You, Hashem, Who heals all flesh and does wonders.

I had always liked it for its simplicity, for its appreciation of the necessity of bodily function. I so wanted to keep my body functioning. And I knew very clearly that I needed God's help. I wanted God to share in the burden to preserve what I had.

I am not a *davener*, one who prays. My husband is. Joe prays three times a day and goes to daily *minyanim*, services, no matter where we are in the world. I often call these services, "the other woman" as Joe is very devoted to attending these services. But I am of a different cloth. When we were dating, he would call on Saturday nights, after Shabbat, and joke, "And which *shul* – synagogue – didn't you go to this week?"

After that first chemo, I realized that I had a need – a need to be more participatory, more emotionally and especially spiritually involved in the process, and the *Asher Yatzar* prayer was the vehicle that immediately came to mind. First, it was very familiar and comfortable. It is in simple, clear Hebrew and it comes right to the point. It had always spoken to me and it expressed both gratitude to God (and hope for successful bodily function.)

By the second taxol treatment, the mediport had been installed in my chest, so there was less prodding and poking, and my arms and hands were needle-free. My glasses were often on the little side table (and not within reach) at Memorial Sloan Kettering's sixth floor, so Joe had both the Hebrew and English text of the prayer enlarged several times so that I could read it comfortably with or without glasses.

As the first drip of taxol entered my system, I took out the 11" X 14" sheet of paper, whispered a little personal prayer first, and then recited the *Asher Yatzar*.

What a comfort it was to have God as my partner! It then became part of the routine: first the hydration, then the antihistamine and then the carboplatin-taxol-*Asher Yatzar* combination. So far, it's been a winning combination.

As of this writing, I have, thank God, been in remission for five years. I hope and pray that I will stay in remission. But if I'm not that fortunate, then I know that *Asher Yatzar* will be my prayer of choice, once again, to see me through the ordeal.

Elohai Neshamah Shenatata Bi

Rabbi Samuel Barth

אֱלֹהַי, נְשָׁמָה שֶׁנָּתַתָּ בִּי טְהוֹרָה הִיא. אַתָּה בְרָאתָהּ, אַתָּה יְצַרְתָּהּ, אַתָּה נְפַחְתָּהּ בִּי, וְאַתָּה מְשַׁמְּרָהּ בְּקִרְבִּי, וְאַתָּה עָתִיד לִטְּלָהּ מִמֶּנִּי, וּלְהַחֲזִירָהּ בִּי לֶעָתִיד לָבוֹא. כָּל זְמַן שֶׁהַנְּשָׁמָה בְקִרְבִּי, מוֹדֶה/מוֹדָה אֲנִי לְפָנֶיךָ, יְיָ אֱלֹהַי וֵאלֹהֵי אֲבוֹתַי, רִבּוֹן כָּל הַמַּעֲשִׂים, אֲדוֹן כָּל הַנְּשָׁמוֹת. בָּרוּךְ אַתָּה יְיָ, הַמַּחֲזִיר נְשָׁמוֹת לִפְגָרִים מֵתִים.

The preliminary prayers recited at synagogue each morning are rarely encountered; even if you arrive 15 minutes after the published starting time for a service that might last more than three hours, you will miss those first important words. This fills me with real sorrow, for within this section of the *siddur* are remarkable, beautiful affirmations and reflections. In *Adon Olam*, the poet entrusts body and soul to God each night. So, in the morning, it is natural to give thanks for one more day of life, and to reflect on who we are as human beings, composed of body and soul.

The prayer *Elohai Neshamah* affirms that the soul (*neshamah*) is breathed into us by God, and that it is pure. Interestingly, the Hebrew word for breath is *neshimah*, so close to the word for soul that the two are intimately connected. The soul is the very breath of life, and as we are aware of our breath, perhaps we approach a point of connection. Careful pronunciation of the Hebrew (using the *mappik* dot [·] at the end of a succession of words) demands equally careful and emphasized breathing. The prayer accepts that, one day, the soul will be taken from the body, affirming that our spiritual life does not end when the body dies—and that the soul as a focal point of our identity will live in eternity.

The early morning may not be the best time for analytic philosophical reflection, but I suggest that it is the best time to affirm deep beliefs and dreams. It is not enough to study theology and philosophy, from Descartes and Maimonides onward, to arrive at an understanding of the relationship between body and soul. We must act, celebrate, and breathe based upon our understanding. The *siddur* invites and inspires us to do just that. (Note that the word *inspire* itself literally means to breathe in.)

The end of the prayer is a blessing that praises God, "who restores the soul to the lifeless, exhausted body." This is well understood in relationship to the last line of *Adon Olam*; we have given ourselves to God through the night (sleep is as one-sixtieth of death), and we find joy in the morning as we feel ourselves renewed, spiritual beings. Our bodies may be infirm, disabled, or challenged in other ways, but our divine likeness is not beheld in the optics of a mirror; rather it is in the *neshamah*, the breath of life.

Elohai Neshamah Shenatata Bi

Rabbi Steven A. Schwarzman

Every single morning, we start off reminding God that our souls are pure. As if God needed a reminder!

The prayer itself thanks God for creating our souls, forming them, blowing them into us, keeping them within us, and one day taking them from us only in order to return them to us in the future.

But I think the reminder is for us, not for God. When we wake up, we remember our failings from the previous day. Reminding ourselves that our souls remain just as pure as the day we were born also reminds us that we can make today more like it can and should be, and that whatever we did wrong yesterday, it needn't stop us from doing the right thing today.

La'asok Bedivrei Torah

Rabbi Steven A. Schwarzman

בָּרוּךְ אַתָּה יְיָ אֱלֹהֵינוּ מֶלֶךְ הָעוֹלָם, אֲשֶׁר קִדְּשָׁנוּ בְּמִצְוֹתָיו, וְצִוָּנוּ לַעֲסוֹק בְּדִבְרֵי תוֹרָה:

וְהַעֲרֶב־נָא יְיָ אֱלֹהֵינוּ אֶת־דִּבְרֵי תוֹרָתְךָ בְּפִינוּ, וּבְפִי עַמְּךָ בֵּית יִשְׂרָאֵל, וְנִהְיֶה אֲנַחְנוּ וְצֶאֱצָאֵינוּ, וְצֶאֱצָאֵי עַמְּךָ בֵּית יִשְׂרָאֵל, כֻּלָּנוּ יוֹדְעֵי שְׁמֶךָ, וְלוֹמְדֵי תוֹרָתֶךָ לִשְׁמָהּ: בָּרוּךְ אַתָּה יְיָ, הַמְלַמֵּד תּוֹרָה לְעַמּוֹ יִשְׂרָאֵל:

בָּרוּךְ אַתָּה יְיָ אֱלֹהֵינוּ מֶלֶךְ הָעוֹלָם, אֲשֶׁר בָּחַר בָּנוּ מִכָּל הָעַמִּים, וְנָתַן לָנוּ אֶת תּוֹרָתוֹ: בָּרוּךְ אַתָּה יְיָ, נוֹתֵן הַתּוֹרָה:

The first of several blessings we say in the morning about Torah is *la'asok bedivrei Torah* – blessing God who has commanded us to occupy ourselves with Torah. But we don't stop there; the prayer continues with a plea to God: make the words of your Torah pleasant in our mouths and the mouth of your people, the House of Israel. And once we are pleading with God to make Torah sweet for us, we don't stop there: we ask God to make us, our children, and all Jews knowers of God's name and learners of God's Torah for its own sake.

It's a fascinating sequence: first we occupy ourselves with Torah. We live Torah. Yes, we study it, too, but it's not just an academic subject. It's a lifestyle. And once Torah becomes part of our lives, perhaps the lens through which we see and live life, it can sweeten our lives. Sharing words of Torah with each other becomes not a burden, but a sweetness. And when our kids see how sweet Torah is – not in theory, but in the lives of their very own parents – then they, too, can become knowers of God's name and learners of God's Torah.

What a beautiful prayer! And no wonder that multiple blessings are needed to cover the vastness of Torah.

La'asok Bedivrei Torah

Linda Friedman

Having been born and raised in the Bronx (in New York City), I attended public school (P.S. 19) from kindergarten to grade 8. I was always a very enthusiastic student and received excellent grades. So, many years later as a grown woman, I could not understand why I occasionally was having a recurrent dream about elementary school.

In my dream, I had received a letter from P.S. 19 saying that I had not properly completed my studies and was required to return to classes there. Of course, being an adult, I pictured myself squeezed into a child's desk surrounded by young children learning the lessons that I seemed to have missed. From time to time, I would find myself in this scenario while I slept, and awoke perplexed by it.

At the age of 32, I moved to Toronto and joined Beth Emeth Bais Yehuda Synagogue. Rabbi Kelman encouraged me to join his Jewish study classes on Tuesday mornings. The classes were held in one of the social halls of the synagogue, and I attended regularly.

One day, the Rabbi wanted to demonstrate the concept of root words in Hebrew on a blackboard, so he took our class to a Hebrew school classroom to use the blackboard. And, lo and behold, there I was, squeezing into a child's desk in the classroom. I suddenly realized the meaning of my recurrent dream!

When I was growing up, both of my brothers were taught about Judaism and learned to read Hebrew in preparation for their Bar Mitzvahs. The possibility of me attending Hebrew school was never even mentioned. I also remembered watching my older cousin on the *bimah* of her synagogue during her Bat Mitzvah ceremony, and feeling that she was so lucky to know how to read the prayers and have the pride of that very special accomplishment.

So, at the age of 32, I realized that my dream meant that indeed my elementary school education wasn't complete. I still needed to go back to "school" to learn all that I missed by not going to Hebrew school as a child.

While I have participated in many informal Jewish study classes at Beth Emeth and later at Shaar Shalom, I finally fulfilled my dream by graduating from a two-year formal Adult Bat Mitzvah program at the age of 58, and I have never had my recurrent dream ever again!

La'asok Bedivrei Torah

Rabbi Samuel Barth

We do not study Torah primarily to find out what God wants us to do, and we certainly do not study our sacred texts to learn history, or medicine. The act of *Talmud Torah*, the studying of Torah, is itself a *mitzvah*, a commandment. As with many commandments (eating *matzah*, putting on *tefillin*, etc.), there is a *berakhah*, a blessing, that precedes the act. In *Siddur Sim Shalom: A Prayerbook for Shabbat, Festivals, and Weekdays*, we find three linked blessings about Torah. The third of these is the familiar blessing recited by those called for an *aliyah* to the public reading of the Torah. The first of the series is in the normal formula, *"Asher kid'shanu bemitzvotav, vetzivanu..."* (God has made us holy with commandments, and has commanded us...), but the conclusion that we might expect ("...to study Torah") is absent; instead, we find the expression "...*la'asok bedivrei Torah*" ("...to occupy ourselves with matters of Torah"). The Hebrew verb is precisely the verb used for describing the way in which we earn a living in the world, our professions and crafts. This blessing invites us to see engagement with Torah as a profession, a craft, no less than anything else that occupies our lives.

The second of the three blessings (*"Ve-ha'arev na"*) begins with an unusual request; usually blessings of petition ask for things that can be touched and observed, such as successful harvests, good health, peace in the world, etc. This blessing ends with praising God as "the One Who teaches Torah to the People Israel," but it begins with an experiential request. It does not ask that we should all be "A" students, mastering a full page of Talmud each day — and a couple of irregular verbs a well. It asks, instead, that we find the words of Torah to be "lovely in our mouths and in the mouths of our children." We do not pray for successful learning, we pray for delightful learning.

This blessing lasts all day; we do not generally need to say the blessings again each time we turn to study Torah. The blessing is followed by a ritualized act of study as we read the words of the Priestly Blessing from the book of Numbers and a short passage from the *Mishnah* and *Gemara*, affirming the radical view that rabbinic texts are Torah no less than words from the Five Books of the Written Torah. Even if we know these excerpts by heart, they are still repeated each day. The growing familiarity with these short passages engages us in a ritual of study; reflecting on these texts and on the words of the *siddur* guides us on the journey from ritual study to study *as* ritual.

Mah Tovu

Rabbi Steven A. Schwarzman

מַה טֹּבוּ אֹהָלֶיךָ יַעֲקֹב, מִשְׁכְּנֹתֶיךָ יִשְׂרָאֵל. וַאֲנִי בְּרֹב חַסְדְּךָ אָבוֹא בֵיתֶךָ, אֶשְׁתַּחֲוֶה אֶל הֵיכַל קָדְשְׁךָ בְּיִרְאָתֶךָ. יְיָ אָהַבְתִּי מְעוֹן בֵּיתֶךָ, וּמְקוֹם מִשְׁכַּן כְּבוֹדֶךָ. וַאֲנִי אֶשְׁתַּחֲוֶה וְאֶכְרָעָה, אֶבְרְכָה לִפְנֵי יְיָ עֹשִׂי. וַאֲנִי, תְפִלָּתִי לְךָ יְיָ, עֵת רָצוֹן, אֱלֹהִים בְּרֹב חַסְדֶּךָ, עֲנֵנִי בֶּאֱמֶת יִשְׁעֶךָ.

As my beloved teacher, Professor Judah Goldin of blessed memory, once wrote (in his book, *The Jewish Expression*), "Upon entering a synagogue it is customary to recite, 'How fair are thy tents, O Jacob, thy dwellings, O Israel!'"

The funny thing is, this quote from the Torah does not come from Moses, or Aaron, or Miriam. It comes from Bilaam, the non-Jewish seer hired to curse Israel by King Balak of Moav. As Prof. Goldin wrote, it was "originally proclaimed by a non-Israelite visionary, long before there was anything like a synagogue in existence."

And we say it every time we walk into a synagogue.

Sometimes real *tikkun* – what we might call a corrective realignment of cosmic forces – takes place when we take something that was said badly, or in a bad context, or by a bad person, and we find a way to transform it willy-nilly into something good.

How goodly are your tents, Jacob, your dwelling places, Israel! According to a *midrash*, this was what came out of Bilaam's mouth, intended as a curse but transformed into a blessing, when he looked down at the Israelite camp and saw that they had lined up their tents so as to ensure each family's privacy. One tent didn't open directly onto another. And this was intentional, so that the people of Israel would retain a sense of decency and propriety even in the informal and difficult conditions of living in the desert.

I don't always think about all this when I walk into shul and say these words. But about 90% of the time, I do. It's a nice reminder that, on the one hand, Judaism is all about decency in all its respects, and that on the other, we don't have a monopoly on wisdom. We start our synagogue prayers by quoting a non-Jew hired to bring about our downfall. And we're still doing it, thousands of years after those words were first spoken.

Birkhot Hashahar

Rabbi Steven A. Schwarzman

בָּרוּךְ אַתָּה יְיָ אֱלֹהֵינוּ מֶלֶךְ הָעוֹלָם, אֲשֶׁר נָתַן לַשֶּׂכְוִי בִינָה, לְהַבְחִין בֵּין יוֹם וּבֵין לָיְלָה:

[1] בָּרוּךְ אַתָּה יְיָ אֱלֹהֵינוּ מֶלֶךְ הָעוֹלָם, שֶׁלֹּא עָשַׂנִי גּוֹי:

בָּרוּךְ אַתָּה יְיָ אֱלֹהֵינוּ מֶלֶךְ הָעוֹלָם, שֶׁלֹּא עָשַׂנִי עָבֶד:

בָּרוּךְ אַתָּה יְיָ אֱלֹהֵינוּ מֶלֶךְ הָעוֹלָם, שֶׁלֹּא עָשַׂנִי אִשָּׁה/שֶׁעָשַׂנִי כִּרְצוֹנוֹ:

בָּרוּךְ אַתָּה יְיָ אֱלֹהֵינוּ מֶלֶךְ הָעוֹלָם, פּוֹקֵחַ עִוְרִים:

בָּרוּךְ אַתָּה יְיָ אֱלֹהֵינוּ מֶלֶךְ הָעוֹלָם, מַלְבִּישׁ עֲרֻמִּים:

בָּרוּךְ אַתָּה יְיָ אֱלֹהֵינוּ מֶלֶךְ הָעוֹלָם, מַתִּיר אֲסוּרִים:

בָּרוּךְ אַתָּה יְיָ אֱלֹהֵינוּ מֶלֶךְ הָעוֹלָם, זוֹקֵף כְּפוּפִים:

בָּרוּךְ אַתָּה יְיָ אֱלֹהֵינוּ מֶלֶךְ הָעוֹלָם, רוֹקַע הָאָרֶץ עַל הַמָּיִם:

בָּרוּךְ אַתָּה יְיָ אֱלֹהֵינוּ מֶלֶךְ הָעוֹלָם, שֶׁעָשָׂה לִי כָּל צָרְכִּי:

בָּרוּךְ אַתָּה יְיָ אֱלֹהֵינוּ מֶלֶךְ הָעוֹלָם הַמֵּכִין מִצְעֲדֵי גָבֶר:

בָּרוּךְ אַתָּה יְיָ אֱלֹהֵינוּ מֶלֶךְ הָעוֹלָם, אוֹזֵר יִשְׂרָאֵל בִּגְבוּרָה:

בָּרוּךְ אַתָּה יְיָ אֱלֹהֵינוּ מֶלֶךְ הָעוֹלָם, עוֹטֵר יִשְׂרָאֵל בְּתִפְאָרָה:

בָּרוּךְ אַתָּה יְיָ אֱלֹהֵינוּ מֶלֶךְ הָעוֹלָם, הַנּוֹתֵן לַיָּעֵף כֹּחַ:

Fourteen. Count 'em, fourteen blessings in a row. Most synagogue services start with these blessings, with the prayers that come before them usually said quietly by the individual pray-ers.

---

[1] Shown here is the text as found in Orthodox *siddurim*. Conservative *siddurim* change this and the following two benedictions from a negative formulation to a positive one. In both formulations, we thank God for making us Jews able to fulfill God's commandments.

They cover a lot of territory, these fourteen blessings. But what they have in common is not the themes each expresses, but the fact that they are blessings. *Barukh atah...barukh atah...barukh atah* – say that fourteen times, and you begin to discern the pattern, even when you are still sleepy. Never mind the details of each blessing, if your still-half-asleep brain can't really process them yet. What counts is *Barukh atah, barukh atah*. We start the public part of our prayers praising God over and over again.

Barukh atah – Blessed are you, Lord our God, Ruler of the Universe. By blessing and praising God over and over, we start our public day by acknowledging God's presence in our lives as our Creator and as our personal God – and by acknowledging that we acknowledge this.

Birkhot Hashahar

Heather G. Stoltz

This piece is part of a series on the weekday morning liturgy. *Birkhot Hashahar* is the first section of the morning service. During this time of day, we are just waking up to the many sights, sounds, and textures of the physical world and we give thanks to God for each of them.

This crazy quilt is made of fabrics of many different colors, weights, and textures to represent the sensory overload we experience upon waking as well as our thankfulness for the ability to experience all our senses in this physical world. The quilting lines meander through the piece and converge at the top to represent our movement through this part of the morning service to a place where we are more able to speak with God.

Yehi Ratzon

Rabbi Samuel Barth

יְהִי רָצוֹן מִלְּפָנֶיךָ, יְיָ אֱלֹהַי וֵאלֹהֵי אֲבוֹתַי, שֶׁתַּצִּילֵנִי הַיּוֹם וּבְכָל יוֹם
מֵעַזֵּי פָנִים וּמֵעַזּוּת פָּנִים, מֵאָדָם רָע, וּמֵחָבֵר רָע, וּמִשָּׁכֵן רָע, וּמִפֶּגַע רָע,
וּמִשָּׂטָן הַמַּשְׁחִית, מִדִּין קָשֶׁה, וּמִבַּעַל דִּין קָשֶׁה, בֵּין שֶׁהוּא בֶן בְּרִית,
וּבֵין שֶׁאֵינוֹ בֶן בְּרִית.

In the preliminary service, there is a short paragraph remarkably written in the first person singular—using "I" rather than "we." In the Talmud (BT Berakhot 16b), there are a number of personal prayers of the Sages, the prayers that they would say at the end of the 'Amidah. This text is attributed to Rabbi Yehudah HaNasi and is inserted at this point in the service because it is similar in theme to the previous paragraph. There is a telling, and sometimes uncomfortable, phrase that begins very innocently, "tatzileini hayom . . . me'azei panim" (save me this day from those with "hard faces" [from the arrogant]). This is a reasonable hope and a fine, if unremarkable, prayer; it would be good to pass a day (or even longer) without encountering others who are arrogant. But that is not the end of the sentence. The prayer of Rabbi Yehudah continues, "ume'azut panim" (and from my own "hard face" [my own arrogance]).

It is easy to see flaws in other people, and to seek to avoid being bothered by these flaws in others. The exquisitely nuanced construction of this phrase by Rabbi Yehudah reminds us that it is precisely that which we dislike most in others that we are most likely to find within ourselves—if we look.

This inner discernment requires that we ask questions, hard and searching questions of ourselves. Perhaps it is no accident that this prayer of Rabbi Yehudah is a preface to one of my favorite paragraphs of the preliminary service—the paragraph that asks of us all a searching series of questions: *"Mah anu, meh hayeinu?"* (Who are we, what is our life?).

The nature of humanity has not changed so much over the centuries and millennia, and it is reassuring and challenging to find in the pages of the *siddur* these phrases that alert us to our own foibles. Abraham Joshua Heschel famously wrote that "prayer is subversive"; perhaps the subversion is of our inner self-deception.

Ribon Kol Ha'olamim

Edwin R. Frankel

לְעוֹלָם יְהֵא אָדָם יְרֵא שָׁמַיִם בְּסֵתֶר וּבַגָּלוּי, וּמוֹדֶה עַל הָאֱמֶת, וְדוֹבֵר
אֱמֶת בִּלְבָבוֹ, וְיַשְׁכֵּם וְיֹאמַר:

רִבּוֹן כָּל הָעוֹלָמִים, לֹא עַל צִדְקוֹתֵינוּ, אֲנַחְנוּ מַפִּילִים תַּחֲנוּנֵינוּ לְפָנֶיךָ,
כִּי עַל רַחֲמֶיךָ הָרַבִּים. מָה אֲנַחְנוּ, מֶה חַיֵּינוּ, מֶה חַסְדֵּנוּ, מַה
צִּדְקוֹתֵינוּ, מַה יְשׁוּעָתֵנוּ, מַה כֹּחֵנוּ, מַה גְּבוּרָתֵנוּ. מַה נֹּאמַר לְפָנֶיךָ, יְיָ
אֱלֹהֵינוּ וֵאלֹהֵי אֲבוֹתֵינוּ, הֲלֹא כָּל הַגִּבּוֹרִים כְּאַיִן לְפָנֶיךָ, וְאַנְשֵׁי הַשֵּׁם
כְּלֹא הָיוּ, וַחֲכָמִים כִּבְלִי מַדָּע, וּנְבוֹנִים כִּבְלִי הַשְׂכֵּל. כִּי רֹב מַעֲשֵׂיהֶם
תֹּהוּ, וִימֵי חַיֵּיהֶם הֶבֶל לְפָנֶיךָ, וּמוֹתַר הָאָדָם מִן הַבְּהֵמָה אָיִן, כִּי הַכֹּל
הָבֶל: אֲבָל אֲנַחְנוּ עַמְּךָ, בְּנֵי בְרִיתֶךָ, בְּנֵי אַבְרָהָם אֹהַבְךָ, שֶׁנִּשְׁבַּעְתָּ לּוֹ
בְּהַר הַמּוֹרִיָּה, זֶרַע יִצְחָק יְחִידוֹ, שֶׁנֶּעֱקַד עַל גַּבֵּי הַמִּזְבֵּחַ, עֲדַת יַעֲקֹב
בִּנְךָ בְּכוֹרֶךָ, שֶׁמֵּאַהֲבָתְךָ שֶׁאָהַבְתָּ אוֹתוֹ, וּמִשִּׂמְחָתְךָ שֶׁשָּׂמַחְתָּ בּוֹ,
קָרָאתָ אֶת שְׁמוֹ יִשְׂרָאֵל וִישֻׁרוּן:

There is no more interesting prayer, in my humble opinion, than that said immediately following *Birkhot Hashahar* during the majority of the year. The words are so significant, that they are also featured in the *Amidah* on *Yamim Noraim*, the Days of Awe.

From childhood, I was taught that the term *tefillah* refers to a reflective act. The root *peh-lamed-lamed* means to see. Thus, to pray, *l'hitpalel*, literally means to introspect. As much as all the prayers of request (*bakashot*) demand prior introspection to be sincere, and prayers of acknowledgement (*hoda'ah*) require awareness of the goodness from which a worshipper has benefited, few prayers are truly introspective or meditative.

Ribon Kol Ha'olamim demands introspection. It is a bold prayer. The Almighty is not initially identified in it as Rock of Israel or any other reference that binds the Godhead with our people. Rather, the prayer, from its initial words, ties God to all that exists, not only in our world/universe, but in the multiple universes that now are already recognized in much science fiction and, some would argue, real science as well.

Moreover, the prayer stresses the transcendence of God. We have no proper deeds powerful enough to cause God to hearken to our pleas. Rather, we rely on God's manifold mercifulness. That too, is a strange combination. If God is transcendent, whence a sense of mercy? Yet if God is immanent, would God not recognize our deservedness for Divine attention?

The most compelling aspect of the prayer is its series of serious questions. Most worshippers read the litany and likely regard the queries as rhetorical. Yet if that is done, their power is sorely lacking. To properly recite this prayer and respond to its lesson would obligate hours of active thought, and to do some from time to time is likely a wonderful exercise in *heshbon nefesh*, taking account of ourselves.

I have no answers for the questions. Each time I grapple with them, my responses tend to change. To me, that is the mark of a vital instrument that holds its value. "What are we? What is our life? What is our piety?" More than read the questions as written, I strive as well to deal with each question in the singular, as if directed to me alone.

Sometimes, while completing the process to personal satisfaction, worshippers are only momentarily permitted to gloat in a sense of accomplishment. More often, they may be chagrined that, despite a sense of accomplishment, when compared to the deeds of the Creator, they are naught. When gloating, the terms of the prayer itself bring worshippers back to earth, for it teaches that "our actions are meaningless, the days of our life, void. Human preeminence over other animals is an illusion."

Yet the prayer then also manages to bolster spirits. After helping us become struck silent by the awe of Divine magnificence, and compelling us to a deep sense of humility, the prayer reminds us that the God of all universes does have a special tie with Israel as partners in a covenant, as heirs of a long and proud tradition from the time of our earliest ancestors. It recalls God's special love for *Yaakov Avinu* (Jacob), and hence for all of his heirs.

The prayer resolutely knocks us down a measure and then carefully reaffirms our special relationship. It proclaims our obligation to extol and thank and glorify the Almighty, and that we are better off for that opportunity.

The downcast cannot properly offer sincere praise; they are too mired in their own misery. The haughty, however, cannot appropriately recognize God's import, until they have been knocked down a peg.

This *tefillah*, thus, for me is the epitome of *tefillah*.

The Baraita of Rabbi Yishmael

Rabbi Steven A. Schwarzman

(א): רַבִּי יִשְׁמָעֵאל אוֹמֵר, בִּשְׁלֹשׁ עֶשְׂרֵה מִדּוֹת הַתּוֹרָה נִדְרֶשֶׁת בָּהֶן
מִקַּל וָחֹמֶר. (ב) וּמִגְּזֵרָה שָׁוָה. (ג) מִבִּנְיַן אָב מִכָּתוּב אֶחָד, וּמִבִּנְיַן אָב
מִשְּׁנֵי כְתוּבִים. (ד) מִכְּלָל וּפְרָט. (ה) וּמִפְּרָט וּכְלָל. (ו) כְּלָל וּפְרָט וּכְלָל ,
אִי אַתָּה דָן אֶלָּא כְּעֵין הַפְּרָט. (ז) מִכְּלָל שֶׁהוּא צָרִיךְ לִפְרָט, וּמִפְּרָט
שֶׁהוּא צָרִיךְ לִכְלָל. (ח) כָּל דָּבָר שֶׁהָיָה בִכְלָל וְיָצָא מִן הַכְּלָל לְלַמֵּד, לֹא
לְלַמֵּד עַל עַצְמוֹ יָצָא, אֶלָּא לְלַמֵּד עַל הַכְּלָל כֻּלּוֹ יָצָא. (ט) כָּל דָּבָר
שֶׁהָיָה בִכְלָל, וְיָצָא לִטְעוֹן טוֹעַן אֶחָד שֶׁהוּא כְעִנְיָנוֹ, יָצָא לְהָקֵל וְלֹא
לְהַחֲמִיר. (י) כָּל דָּבָר שֶׁהָיָה בִכְלָל וְיָצָא לִטְעוֹן טוֹעַן אַחֵר שֶׁלֹּא כְעִנְיָנוֹ,
יָצָא לְהָקֵל וּלְהַחֲמִיר. (יא) כָּל דָּבָר שֶׁהָיָה בִכְלָל וְיָצָא לִדּוֹן בַּדָּבָר
הֶחָדָשׁ, אִי אַתָּה יָכוֹל לְהַחֲזִירוֹ לִכְלָלוֹ, עַד שֶׁיַּחֲזִירֶנּוּ הַכָּתוּב לִכְלָלוֹ
בְּפֵירוּשׁ. יב דָּבָר הַלָּמֵד מֵעִנְיָנוֹ. וְדָבָר הַלָּמֵד מִסּוֹפוֹ. יג וְכֵן (נ"א וְכָאן)
שְׁנֵי כְתוּבִים הַמַּכְחִישִׁים זֶה אֶת זֶה, עַד שֶׁיָּבֹא הַכָּתוּב הַשְּׁלִישִׁי
וְיַכְרִיעַ בֵּינֵיהֶם :

This rabbinic text from the beginning of the *Sifra* is studied every day. It is a list of Rabbi Yishmael's hermeneutical rules – that is, rules of interpretation – for deriving *halakhah* from the text of the Torah. It's not easy stuff, most of it. Sure, anyone gets *mikal vahomer* – literally, from light to heavy or from easy to severe. If it's illegal to go five miles above the speed limit, it's certainly illegal to go twenty miles above the limit.

But many of the other rules are far more complicated. Or so they seem to my still-sleepy brain during morning *minyan*. I know that if I were to take the time to reflect on the meaning of each one, I would get it. But there's little time for such pondering during a weekday *minyan*.

And so I read Rabbi Yishmael's rules as something of a placeholder. They're important, I know, because they're nothing less than what constitutes legitimate interpretation of Scripture in the determination of Jewish law and what doesn't. But I am happy, in those early mornings, to give Rabbi Yishmael credit for getting the rules right even when I'm not always able to take the time to get to the bottom of what he's saying. It's a matter of faith.

Oddly enough, if I'm late, this is not a prayer I skip. I need my daily chat with the good rabbi of a couple of thousand years ago, even if I don't always understand what he says to me before the morning's coffee.

Perhaps this thought can be helpful to those struggling to understand the meaning of another prayer. Sometimes it's okay to pray the prayer anyway. There will be days when you'll get it more, and days when you may not get as much of it. But have faith...and keep the conversation alive with the text of the prayer. That, too, is faith.

Kaddish Derabanan

Rabbi Steven A. Schwarzman

יִתְגַּדַּל וְיִתְקַדַּשׁ שְׁמֵהּ רַבָּא. בְּעָלְמָא דִּי בְרָא כִרְעוּתֵיהּ, וְיַמְלִיךְ מַלְכוּתֵיהּ בְּחַיֵּיכוֹן וּבְיוֹמֵיכוֹן וּבְחַיֵּי דְכָל בֵּית יִשְׂרָאֵל. בַּעֲגָלָא וּבִזְמַן קָרִיב וְאִמְרוּ אָמֵן :

יְהֵא שְׁמֵהּ רַבָּא מְבָרַךְ לְעָלַם וּלְעָלְמֵי עָלְמַיָּא :

יִתְבָּרַךְ וְיִשְׁתַּבַּח וְיִתְפָּאַר וְיִתְרוֹמַם וְיִתְנַשֵּׂא וְיִתְהַדָּר וְיִתְעַלֶּה וְיִתְהַלָּל שְׁמֵהּ דְּקֻדְשָׁא בְּרִיךְ הוּא לְעֵלָּא (בעשי״ת וּלְעֵלָּא מִכָּל) מִן כָּל בִּרְכָתָא וְשִׁירָתָא תֻּשְׁבְּחָתָא וְנֶחֱמָתָא, דַּאֲמִירָן בְּעָלְמָא, וְאִמְרוּ אָמֵן :

עַל יִשְׂרָאֵל וְעַל רַבָּנָן, וְעַל תַּלְמִידֵיהוֹן וְעַל כָּל תַּלְמִידֵי תַלְמִידֵיהוֹן, וְעַל כָּל מָאן דְּעָסְקִין בְּאוֹרַיְתָא, דִּי בְאַתְרָא הָדֵין וְדִי בְכָל אֲתַר וַאֲתַר. יְהֵא לְהוֹן וּלְכוֹן שְׁלָמָא רַבָּא, חִנָּא וְחִסְדָּא וְרַחֲמִין, וְחַיִּין אֲרִיכִין, וּמְזוֹנֵי רְוִיחֵי, וּפֻרְקָנָא, מִן קֳדָם אֲבוּהוֹן דִּי בִשְׁמַיָּא וְאִמְרוּ אָמֵן.

יְהֵא שְׁלָמָא רַבָּא מִן שְׁמַיָּא, וְחַיִּים טוֹבִים עָלֵינוּ וְעַל כָּל יִשְׂרָאֵל וְאִמְרוּ אָמֵן.

עֹשֶׂה שָׁלוֹם בִּמְרוֹמָיו הוּא בְּרַחֲמָיו יַעֲשֶׂה שָׁלוֹם עָלֵינוּ וְעַל כָּל יִשְׂרָאֵל, וְאִמְרוּ אָמֵן :

After studying a rabbinic text – customarily, it has to be a *rabbinic* text, not just, say, Bible – we recite *Kaddish Derabanan*, the Rabbis' Kaddish, if a *minyan* is present. It starts out the same as the more familiar Mourner's Kaddish, but has an added paragraph asking for peace, God's grace and mercy, long life, ample sustenance, and salvation from God in heaven for – well, for all Israel, but then specifically for the Rabbis, their students, their students' students, and all who occupy themselves with Torah, wherever they may be.

The prayer, or at least this part of it, is bookended by all Israel and all who occupy themselves with Torah. But inside those bookends are rabbis and their students.

Maybe this strikes you as preferential treatment, because after all it is the Rabbis who wrote the prayers that are now in the siddur. But I can tell you as a rabbi that there are plenty of times when we rabbis need God's peace, grace, mercy, long life, sustenance, and ultimately salvation.

We need God's blessing of peace within ourselves as we struggle to know what is best for the communities we lead. We need God's peace in our relations with members of our communities and in their relations with each other. We need God's grace to shine on our endeavors, because God knows how our communities can sometimes judge us. We need God's mercy on us, and we need to share that mercy with others when we might be inclined to focus instead on justice and the law. We need long life in order to begin to tackle our endless to-do lists, because there is so much work to do in helping Jews live fuller, deeper Jewish lives. We need sustenance for ourselves and for our families. And in the end, when we have done the best we can, we need God's salvation, because even our best will include some failures and missed opportunities.

And this is a prayer that not only rabbis say. The entire congregation says it. Whatever shortcomings rabbis have, their communities know that they need rabbinic leadership to sustain themselves as Jewish communities. It is a prayer for everyone's benefit.

Chapter 3
Pesukei Dezimrah – Verses of Song

When I explain the Shabbat morning service to non-Jewish visitors in the synagogue for a bar or bat mitzvah, I describe Pesukei Dezimrah as (mostly) a series of psalms that we chant or sing in order to prepare ourselves for the actual morning service that follows.

We don't rush into serious conversation with our fellow humans. So why would we think that we could rush into deep prayer with God without first preparing for the conversation?

– Rabbi Steven A. Schwarzman

Pesukei Dezimrah

Heather G. Stoltz

This piece is part of a series on the weekday morning liturgy. *Pesukei Dezimrah* is a section near the beginning of the morning service made up of several psalms. This part of the service is designed to bring us from the physical world into the spiritual realm where we can communicate with God.

The physical world to which we wake is represented by the heavier textured fabrics at the bottom of this piece. As we move through the recitation of psalms, the fabrics transition slowly to lighter fabrics and finally reach the sheers which represent the spiritual world. From there, we are ready to speak to God in prayer.

Barukh She'amar

Rabbi Steven A. Schwarzman

בָּרוּךְ שֶׁאָמַר וְהָיָה הָעוֹלָם, בָּרוּךְ הוּא, בָּרוּךְ עֹשֶׂה בְרֵאשִׁית, בָּרוּךְ
אוֹמֵר וְעוֹשֶׂה, בָּרוּךְ גּוֹזֵר וּמְקַיֵּם, בָּרוּךְ מְרַחֵם עַל הָאָרֶץ, בָּרוּךְ מְרַחֵם
עַל הַבְּרִיּוֹת, בָּרוּךְ מְשַׁלֵּם שָׂכָר טוֹב לִירֵאָיו, בָּרוּךְ חַי לָעַד וְקַיָּם לָנֶצַח,
בָּרוּךְ פּוֹדֶה וּמַצִּיל, בָּרוּךְ שְׁמוֹ

The preliminaries of the morning service are behind
us. Now we begin the longest section of the service,
songs of praise taken primarily from the Book of
Psalms. *Barukh she'amar* – blessed is the one who
spoke and the world came into being. *Barukh oseh
vereishit* – blessed is the one who continually does the
work of Creation. Blessed, blessed, blessed is God
who has mercy on the world, who has mercy on this
world's creatures, who amply rewards the God-
fearing, who lives forever and is established for
eternity, who redeems and saves. Blessed is God's
name.

It's a nice way to start the day, reflecting not on our
own blessings, but on blessing itself.

Barukh She'amar

Heather G. Stoltz

Inspired by the words from the morning prayers *"Barukh she'amar v'hayah ha'olam* – Blessed is the One who spoke the world into being," this quilt depicts several people throughout history who have changed the world through speech. A box that reads "your photo here" asks what the viewer will say to change the world.

Barukh She'amar

Heather G. Stoltz

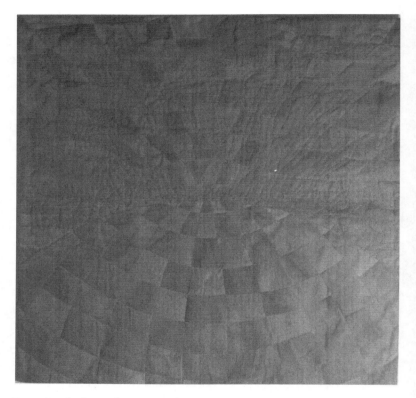

Inspired by the words from the morning prayers *"Barukh she'amar v'hayah ha'olam* – Blessed is the One who spoke the world into being," this quilt shows the creation of the heavens and the earth through God's light/speech/power, which is represented by the burst of orange.

Mizmor Letodah (Psalm 100)

Rabbi Samuel Barth

מִזְמוֹר לְתוֹדָה, הָרִיעוּ לַיְיָ כָּל הָאָרֶץ: עִבְדוּ אֶת יְיָ בְּשִׂמְחָה, בֹּאוּ לְפָנָיו בִּרְנָנָה: דְּעוּ כִּי יְיָ הוּא אֱלֹהִים הוּא עָשָׂנוּ, וְלֹא אֲנַחְנוּ, עַמּוֹ וְצֹאן מַרְעִיתוֹ: בֹּאוּ שְׁעָרָיו בְּתוֹדָה, חֲצֵרֹתָיו בִּתְהִלָּה, הוֹדוּ לוֹ בָּרְכוּ שְׁמוֹ: כִּי טוֹב יְיָ לְעוֹלָם חַסְדּוֹ, וְעַד דֹּר וָדֹר אֱמוּנָתוֹ:

I recall reading *The Adventures of Tom Sawyer* while in elementary school and being stumped by a description of the powerful singing in church of "Old Hundred." What might this "Old Hundred" be, and why was it being sung in church with such fervor? Eventually, I found out that this was Psalm 100, and was sung by the community as it learned that Tom Sawyer was alive, and had mischievously staged his own disappearance.

Within this short psalm is a simple and powerful command: *"Ivdu et Adonai b'simhah!"* (Serve God with joy!), and it is the attempt to fulfill the teaching that has inspired visionaries over the generations to seek renewal and fervor within the structures of Jewish worship. Jewish worship is seen as *avodah* (service), just as the priestly rituals of the Temple are cast as *ha'avodah shebalev* (service of the heart). Our verse from Psalm 100 makes a demand beyond even the concept of *kavanah* (intention)—it demands that we find joy in our worship.

There are certainly many among the Jewish People who see the prayers as rote duty, in which we express the thanks and praise that are due to God. But it is difficult to find joy in carrying out a rote duty. Hasidic masters from the Baal Shem Tov (the founder of Hasidism) onward have turned to this teaching over and over as the basis for introducing ecstatic song, and even dancing, into an otherwise serious order of worship.

The teaching is no less applicable in our own times, and many of the innovations in modern Jewish worship can be understood in its light. For some, there is true joy in new words—new poetry that explores and deepens the themes of worship. The new prayer books of the Reform and Conservative movements (*Mishkan T'filah, Siddur Sim Shalom,* and *Mahzor Lev Shalem*) are wonderful exemplars of attempts to find poetry that stirs the heart and mind alike. A wonderful mix of new and old sounds, classic *hazzanut* juxtaposed with Israeli compositions, and traditional *nusah* and *nigunim* of diverse Hasidic courts have come to adorn modern Jewish worship. Sometimes with instrumentation and sometimes *a cappella*, there is an array of joyful sounds of praise to be heard in our synagogues. This, in so many places, is the true sound of "Old Hundred," the sound of serving God with joy.

Mizmor Letodah (Psalm 100)

Rabbi Steven A. Schwarzman

Among the many psalms we include in our daily prayers is this one, Psalm 100. And perhaps the odd thing about it is when we do *not* include it: not on the morning before Yom Kippur, not on the morning before Passover, and not on any of the days of Passover.

The reason for this is that this psalm, as its superscription or title indicates, was recited in the Temple in Jerusalem during the thanksgiving – *todah* – sacrifice. And that sacrifice included bread – specifically, leavened bread.

That sacrifice would not be offered on the days listed here. Why? Because there was a danger that the leavened bread would remain as Passover began, or that it would remain as Yom Kippur began, both times when it could not be eaten. And offerings should not go to waste.

Today, even when we only say the psalm as a prayer, we maintain the memory of how it was used in the Temple. On the days when *they* wouldn't say it, because they wouldn't offer the accompanying sacrifice, *we* don't say it.

I don't think this is just a mechanical memory, a mere vestige of what once was. So much of rabbinic

Judaism actively memorializes the Temple practices that preceded it. And every morning, when we either say this psalm or purposefully refrain from saying it, we keep alive a memory of how our ancestors worshipped God. We don't toss it out as irrelevant, because even though we no longer offer sacrifices, refraining from saying *Mizmor Letodah* on *erev Pesah* and during *Pesah* and on *erev Yom Kippur* reminds us, the way it reminded our ancestors, that this morning is not like all other mornings.

And even an offering of prayer should not go to waste.

Lamenatzeah Mizmor Ledavid – Psalm 19 (Shabbat)

Rabbi Perry Raphael Rank

לַמְנַצֵּחַ מִזְמוֹר לְדָוִד: יַעַנְךָ יְיָ בְּיוֹם צָרָה, יְשַׂגֶּבְךָ שֵׁם אֱלֹהֵי יַעֲקֹב: יִשְׁלַח עֶזְרְךָ מִקֹּדֶשׁ, וּמִצִּיּוֹן יִסְעָדֶךָּ: יִזְכֹּר כָּל מִנְחֹתֶיךָ, וְעוֹלָתְךָ יְדַשְּׁנֶה סֶלָה: יִתֶּן לְךָ כִלְבָבֶךָ, וְכָל עֲצָתְךָ יְמַלֵּא: נְרַנְּנָה בִּישׁוּעָתֶךָ, וּבְשֵׁם אֱלֹהֵינוּ נִדְגֹּל, יְמַלֵּא יְיָ כָּל מִשְׁאֲלוֹתֶיךָ: עַתָּה יָדַעְתִּי, כִּי הוֹשִׁיעַ יְיָ מְשִׁיחוֹ, יַעֲנֵהוּ מִשְּׁמֵי קָדְשׁוֹ, בִּגְבוּרוֹת יֵשַׁע יְמִינוֹ: אֵלֶּה בָרֶכֶב, וְאֵלֶּה בַסּוּסִים, וַאֲנַחְנוּ בְּשֵׁם יְיָ אֱלֹהֵינוּ נַזְכִּיר: הֵמָּה כָּרְעוּ וְנָפָלוּ, וַאֲנַחְנוּ קַמְנוּ וַנִּתְעוֹדָד: יְיָ הוֹשִׁיעָה, הַמֶּלֶךְ יַעֲנֵנוּ בְיוֹם קָרְאֵנוּ:

"There is no utterance, there are no words, whose sound goes unheard."(Psalm 19:4)

Within the silence of the cosmos is an incessant chattering. The chattering is non-verbal, to be sure, but every meteor and comet, and every star and planet tells us its life story. We are only beginning to decipher their beautiful messages, and what we know as compared with what we don't should humble us for centuries to come.

That God has designed a universe that so readily exposes itself is both a miracle and a blessing. And so it is no wonder that Psalm 19:4 should be recited as part of the *Pesukei Dezimrah* each Shabbat morning. It is a verse that focuses our attention on the mysteries of the universe. On the day when God "rests," we acknowledge that the silence of the cosmos is rich in Torah, that is, the truths that make up our universe.

For millions of years, these messages were monologues spoken into an empty auditorium. But when humanity matured to the point where those messages could be identified and decoded, those lonely speeches became the soaring oratory of Heaven's hosts.

For the spiritually awakened, it has never been clearer that "[t]he heavens declare the glory of God" (Psalm 19:2). The celestial bodies utter nothing, and the structures of heaven do not speak, yet the silence of the cosmos is filled with wonder as each meteor and comet, and every star and planet, praises the One who brought it into being, as their life story continues to unfold in a universe that is forever in motion and forever evolving.

Ashrei

Rabbi Steven A. Schwarzman

אַשְׁרֵי יוֹשְׁבֵי בֵיתֶךָ, עוֹד יְהַלְלוּךָ סֶּלָה: אַשְׁרֵי הָעָם שֶׁכָּכָה לּוֹ, אַשְׁרֵי
הָעָם שֶׁיְיָ אֱלֹהָיו: תְּהִלָּה לְדָוִד, אֲרוֹמִמְךָ אֱלוֹהַי הַמֶּלֶךְ, וַאֲבָרְכָה שִׁמְךָ
לְעוֹלָם וָעֶד: בְּכָל יוֹם אֲבָרְכֶךָ, וַאֲהַלְלָה שִׁמְךָ לְעוֹלָם וָעֶד: גָּדוֹל יְיָ
וּמְהֻלָּל מְאֹד, וְלִגְדֻלָּתוֹ אֵין חֵקֶר: דּוֹר לְדוֹר יְשַׁבַּח מַעֲשֶׂיךָ, וּגְבוּרֹתֶיךָ
יַגִּידוּ: הֲדַר כְּבוֹד הוֹדֶךָ, וְדִבְרֵי נִפְלְאֹתֶיךָ אָשִׂיחָה: וֶעֱזוּז נוֹרְאוֹתֶיךָ
יֹאמֵרוּ וּגְדֻלָּתְךָ אֲסַפְּרֶנָּה: זֵכֶר רַב טוּבְךָ יַבִּיעוּ, וְצִדְקָתְךָ יְרַנֵּנוּ: חַנּוּן
וְרַחוּם יְיָ, אֶרֶךְ אַפַּיִם וּגְדָל חָסֶד: טוֹב יְיָ לַכֹּל, וְרַחֲמָיו עַל כָּל מַעֲשָׂיו:
יוֹדוּךָ יְיָ כָּל מַעֲשֶׂיךָ, וַחֲסִידֶיךָ יְבָרְכוּכָה: כְּבוֹד מַלְכוּתְךָ יֹאמֵרוּ,
וּגְבוּרָתְךָ יְדַבֵּרוּ: לְהוֹדִיעַ לִבְנֵי הָאָדָם גְּבוּרֹתָיו, וּכְבוֹד הֲדַר מַלְכוּתוֹ:
מַלְכוּתְךָ מַלְכוּת כָּל עֹלָמִים, וּמֶמְשַׁלְתְּךָ בְּכָל דֹּר וָדֹר: סוֹמֵךְ יְיָ לְכָל
הַנֹּפְלִים, וְזוֹקֵף לְכָל הַכְּפוּפִים: עֵינֵי כֹל אֵלֶיךָ יְשַׂבֵּרוּ, וְאַתָּה נוֹתֵן לָהֶם
אֶת אָכְלָם בְּעִתּוֹ: פּוֹתֵחַ אֶת יָדֶךָ, וּמַשְׂבִּיעַ לְכָל חַי רָצוֹן: צַדִּיק יְיָ בְּכָל
דְּרָכָיו, וְחָסִיד בְּכָל מַעֲשָׂיו: קָרוֹב יְיָ לְכָל קֹרְאָיו, לְכֹל אֲשֶׁר יִקְרָאֻהוּ
בֶאֱמֶת: רְצוֹן יְרֵאָיו יַעֲשֶׂה, וְאֶת שַׁוְעָתָם יִשְׁמַע וְיוֹשִׁיעֵם: שׁוֹמֵר יְיָ אֶת
כָּל אֹהֲבָיו, וְאֵת כָּל הָרְשָׁעִים יַשְׁמִיד: תְּהִלַּת יְיָ יְדַבֶּר פִּי, וִיבָרֵךְ כָּל
בָּשָׂר שֵׁם קָדְשׁוֹ, לְעוֹלָם וָעֶד: וַאֲנַחְנוּ נְבָרֵךְ יָהּ, מֵעַתָּה וְעַד עוֹלָם,
הַלְלוּיָהּ:

What's so special about *Ashrei*, the Talmud wants to
know, so special that we recite it no fewer than three
times a day – twice in the morning, and once more in
the afternoon? Is it because it's an acrostic, going from
alef to *tav*? Well, there are two problems with that.
First, it's missing a verse, apparently. There is no
verse in *Ashrei* that starts with the letter *nun*. And
second, if it's acrostics you like, there are other psalms
with far more impressive acrostic feats, like Psalm 119
with no fewer than *eight* verses for each letter.

What the Talmud, in tractate Berakhot, likes about
Ashrei is that it is an acrostic *and* that it includes what
is the *peh* verse: *poteah et yadekha umasbia lekhol hai*

ratzon. You open your hand and nourish all life with what it desires.

This is what makes *Ashrei* special?

We moderns, at least in developed countries, tend to take food for granted. If it's not in the refrigerator, it's in the supermarket or in the restaurant, and most of us do not know and have never known true hunger.

But this is not universally so today, and in all but modern times, humans have not had the food security that most of us have now in the West.

When you depend upon God for food – when the vagaries of life make it impossible to know for sure where your next meal is coming from – then recognizing that, ultimately, all food comes from God is a powerful recognition, indeed.

In fact, as Rabbi Amy Eilberg once pointed out when she taught a class on *Ashrei*, we need to remember that this text in the *siddur* is a prayer. That is, it's not necessarily a description of the present so much as a plea for the future to be more like what the verses of the psalm depict.

And this makes it a powerful prayer, indeed. Have trouble saying that God guards all the faithful but punishes the wicked? Or that all those who dwell in God's house are happy? How about that every generation will praise God's works and tell of God's mighty acts? Switch the tense, and make this a prayer for how things *should* be instead of how they necessarily are.

When you do this, God becomes near, indeed, to all who call in truth. And we become aware of our own responsibilities to help make this prayer come true, from *alef* to *tav*.

Ashrei

Linda Friedman

In gratitude, "every day I will praise You." To others, "I will extol You." But it is very reassuring to me to know that "the Lord is gracious and full of compassion, exceedingly patient, abounding in love" and "is near to all who call – to all who call upon the Lord in truth."

In all humility, I need to know these attributes of God, since I am far from perfect and I need His help to have strength.

Halleluyah! Psalm 147

Rabbi Steven A. Schwarzman

הַלְלוּיָהּ, כִּי טוֹב זַמְּרָה אֱלֹהֵינוּ, כִּי נָעִים נָאוָה תְהִלָּה: בּוֹנֵה יְרוּשָׁלַיִם
יְיָ, נִדְחֵי יִשְׂרָאֵל יְכַנֵּס: הָרוֹפֵא לִשְׁבוּרֵי לֵב, וּמְחַבֵּשׁ לְעַצְּבוֹתָם: מוֹנֶה
מִסְפָּר לַכּוֹכָבִים לְכֻלָּם שֵׁמוֹת יִקְרָא: גָּדוֹל אֲדוֹנֵינוּ וְרַב כֹּחַ, לִתְבוּנָתוֹ
אֵין מִסְפָּר: מְעוֹדֵד עֲנָוִים יְיָ, מַשְׁפִּיל רְשָׁעִים עֲדֵי אָרֶץ: עֱנוּ לַיְיָ
בְּתוֹדָה, זַמְּרוּ לֵאלֹהֵינוּ בְכִנּוֹר: הַמְכַסֶּה שָׁמַיִם בְּעָבִים, הַמֵּכִין לָאָרֶץ
מָטָר הַמַּצְמִיחַ הָרִים חָצִיר: נוֹתֵן לִבְהֵמָה לַחְמָהּ, לִבְנֵי עֹרֵב אֲשֶׁר
יִקְרָאוּ: לֹא בִגְבוּרַת הַסּוּס יֶחְפָּץ, לֹא בְשׁוֹקֵי הָאִישׁ יִרְצֶה: רוֹצֶה יְיָ
אֶת יְרֵאָיו, אֶת הַמְיַחֲלִים לְחַסְדּוֹ: שַׁבְּחִי יְרוּשָׁלַיִם אֶת יְיָ, הַלְלִי אֱלֹהַיִךְ
צִיּוֹן: כִּי חִזַּק בְּרִיחֵי שְׁעָרָיִךְ, בֵּרַךְ בָּנַיִךְ בְּקִרְבֵּךְ: הַשָּׂם גְּבוּלֵךְ שָׁלוֹם,
חֵלֶב חִטִּים יַשְׂבִּיעֵךְ: הַשֹּׁלֵחַ אִמְרָתוֹ אָרֶץ, עַד מְהֵרָה יָרוּץ דְּבָרוֹ: הַנֹּתֵן
שֶׁלֶג כַּצָּמֶר, כְּפוֹר כָּאֵפֶר יְפַזֵּר: מַשְׁלִיךְ קַרְחוֹ כְפִתִּים, לִפְנֵי קָרָתוֹ מִי
יַעֲמוֹד: יִשְׁלַח דְּבָרוֹ וְיַמְסֵם, יַשֵּׁב רוּחוֹ יִזְּלוּ מָיִם: מַגִּיד דְּבָרָיו לְיַעֲקֹב,
חֻקָּיו וּמִשְׁפָּטָיו לְיִשְׂרָאֵל: לֹא עָשָׂה כֵן לְכָל גּוֹי, וּמִשְׁפָּטִים בַּל יְדָעוּם,
הַלְלוּיָהּ:

Praise God, cries the Psalmist, because it's good to sing to our God. God constantly builds Jerusalem, and will bring in the downcast of Israel.

Building Jerusalem and bringing in the downcast of Israel – that's *hashgahah* – divine providence – on a national level. But then the psalm turns directly from the national to the personal: God is the Healer of Shattered Hearts, as Rabbi David Wolpe's book by that name attests, Who binds up their wounds.

We take comfort in national joys. So much of Judaism is oriented to the group. We need a *minyan* of ten people to be able to say all the prayers; without it, we are incomplete and so must be our prayers. Even at meals, the *zimun* (introduction) to *birkat hamazon* (grace after meals) takes on a fuller form when we eat with two others, even fuller when we eat with nine others, and, according to the Talmud, fuller still with greater numbers.

But we are not just part of something larger than ourselves, though we are also that. We also count as individuals, and it is God who counts us. God not only cares when our hearts are breaking, but actively helps us find healing. God binds up our wounds.

The wounds of life still happen. To pretend otherwise would be foolish. But God is there to help us heal from those wounds, and that is a great comfort. Not only are we not alone in our sufferings, we will receive God's help when we work to heal ourselves from those sufferings.

And perhaps the first dose of this medicine comes in the very next line: not only does God's providence extend to Israel and Jerusalem, nor only to us as individuals, but also to the entire cosmos: God knows the numbers of the stars, calling each one by name. We are part of a universe that is not left unattended. Our own part in it may be small, but that does not diminish our importance to God. The stars count, and so do we.

Kol Haneshamah Tehallel Yah – Psalm 150

Rabbi Samuel Barth

הַלְלוּיָהּ, הַלְלוּ אֵל בְּקָדְשׁוֹ, הַלְלוּהוּ בִּרְקִיעַ עֻזּוֹ. הַלְלוּהוּ בִגְבוּרֹתָיו,
הַלְלוּהוּ כְּרֹב גֻּדְלוֹ. הַלְלוּהוּ בְּתֵקַע שׁוֹפָר, הַלְלוּהוּ בְּנֵבֶל וְכִנּוֹר. הַלְלוּהוּ
בְתֹף וּמָחוֹל, הַלְלוּהוּ בְּמִנִּים וְעֻגָב. הַלְלוּהוּ בְצִלְצְלֵי שָׁמַע, הַלְלוּהוּ
בְצִלְצְלֵי תְרוּעָה. כֹּל הַנְּשָׁמָה תְּהַלֵּל יָהּ הַלְלוּיָהּ. כֹּל הַנְּשָׁמָה תְּהַלֵּל יָהּ
הַלְלוּיָהּ.

This is the final verse of Psalm 150—the culmination
of the book of Psalms. Every day our set liturgy
includes the final six psalms (145 through 150), and,
to my personal sorrow, the pacing of the so-called
"preliminary service" generally allows a couple of
minutes (at most) for a rushed recitation of these
classic and profound poetic texts. Fortunately, in
many communities—at least on Shabbat, and even on
weekdays—a little more time is allowed for Psalm
150. We find a glorious array of musical
interpretations of the text that exemplify the diverse
approaches to religious music of contemporary
Jewish life.

The text of the psalm is deceptively simple; it can be
seen purely as a list of the musical instruments
engaged in ancient ritual celebrations: harp, cymbals,
shofar, lute, drums, etc. But it offers and invites far
more. Its beginning calls for God to be praised "in
God's holy place, [and] in the highest heavens." The
"holy place" is the Temple in Jerusalem, an entirely
corporeal locale, while the "highest heavens" are

transcendent, far beyond our world. The musical instruments represent corporeal praise, but the psalm goes further, seeking praise not only originating in fabricated instruments, but from *kol haneshamah*, the very breath of life itself. The word *neshamah* has evolved to mean "soul," but in biblical Hebrew it means "breath," as in "the breath of life" (Gen. 2:7).

Psalm 150 offers parallel and paradoxical understandings of God and the way that we praise God. We have corporeal, tangible places where we seek (or even locate) the divine, our synagogues no less than the ancient Temple; but the "real" location of the divine transcends our structures. We look to praise God with our instruments, our words, our voices—but the truest praise transcends these—looking to the universal, the breath, the soul. In the words of Rabbi Dr. Jonathan Magonet,

> *It is not the Jewish People alone who are called upon to praise God, but every soul, every living creature that knows God as the source of its existence.*

Vayosha (Exodus 14:30-31)

Rabbi Steven A. Schwarzman

וַיּוֹשַׁע יְיָ בַּיּוֹם הַהוּא אֶת יִשְׂרָאֵל מִיַּד מִצְרָיִם וַיַּרְא יִשְׂרָאֵל אֶת מִצְרַיִם מֵת עַל שְׂפַת הַיָּם : וַיַּרְא יִשְׂרָאֵל אֶת הַיָּד הַגְּדֹלָה אֲשֶׁר עָשָׂה יְיָ בְּמִצְרַיִם וַיִּירְאוּ הָעָם אֶת יְיָ וַיַּאֲמִינוּ בַּיְיָ וּבְמֹשֶׁה עַבְדּוֹ :

Just before we recite or sing the Song at the Sea, we read its introductory text from Exodus: God saved Israel on that day from Egypt. Israel saw Egypt dead on the shore of the sea. And Israel saw the mighty hand with which God dealt with Egypt. The people feared God and were faithful to God and to Moses his servant.

Of course, that's not how you'll usually see that last sentence translated; most of the time, *vayaminu* gets translated as "believed in" or "had faith in." But it's not about that kind of faith; it's not about suddenly believing in God and Moses when they didn't before.

It's actually about *being* faithful, about fidelity. It's about overcoming their well-documented tendency to slip into something less than that. Throughout Israelite history, when the prophets would rail against the idolatry that the archaeologists have discovered material remains of, it's not that the people didn't *believe* in God.

We often know what's right and what's wrong; it's acting upon that knowledge that often seems to be the problem.

And the Torah, from which this text is taken, is not about Sunday School heroes who are perfect. It's about regular people, sometimes *very* regular people, who fail in the same ways that we often fail.

And this selection from Exodus is here to remind us of this, and that even our very regular ancestors were, at least on this occasion, able to overcome their human weaknesses and for once be faithful to God, leaving behind any desire to cover all the bases by also worshipping other gods.

When the Torah gives us messages like this, they are made all the more powerful by their very reality, by their resemblance to the kinds of situations we face ourselves.

Vayosha...bayom hahu – on that day, God saved Israel, and on that day, Israel was faithful. It doesn't happen every day, just as we are not faithful every day. But from this prayer we learn that we can learn to be faithful, just as our ancestors did. It's a human miracle that perhaps parallels God's miracle of splitting the sea.

Az Yashir Moshe (Exodus 15:1-18)

Gayle Golden

אָז יָשִׁיר מֹשֶׁה וּבְנֵי יִשְׂרָאֵל אֶת הַשִּׁירָה הַזֹּאת לַיְיָ, וַיֹּאמְרוּ לֵאמֹר: אָשִׁירָה לַיְיָ כִּי גָאֹה גָּאָה סוּס וְרֹכְבוֹ רָמָה בַיָּם: עָזִּי וְזִמְרָת יָהּ וַיְהִי לִי לִישׁוּעָה זֶה אֵלִי וְאַנְוֵהוּ אֱלֹהֵי אָבִי וַאֲרֹמְמֶנְהוּ: יְיָ אִישׁ מִלְחָמָה יְיָ שְׁמוֹ: מַרְכְּבֹת פַּרְעֹה וְחֵילוֹ יָרָה בַיָּם, וּמִבְחַר שָׁלִשָׁיו טֻבְּעוּ בְיַם סוּף: תְּהֹמֹת יְכַסְיֻמוּ יָרְדוּ בִמְצוֹלֹת כְּמוֹ אָבֶן: יְמִינְךָ יְיָ נֶאְדָּרִי בַּכֹּחַ, יְמִינְךָ יְיָ תִּרְעַץ אוֹיֵב: וּבְרֹב גְּאוֹנְךָ תַּהֲרֹס קָמֶיךָ תְּשַׁלַּח חֲרֹנְךָ יֹאכְלֵמוֹ כַּקַּשׁ: וּבְרוּחַ אַפֶּיךָ נֶעֶרְמוּ מַיִם נִצְּבוּ כְמוֹ נֵד נֹזְלִים, קָפְאוּ תְהֹמֹת בְּלֶב יָם: אָמַר אוֹיֵב אֶרְדֹּף אַשִּׂיג אֲחַלֵּק שָׁלָל תִּמְלָאֵמוֹ נַפְשִׁי, אָרִיק חַרְבִּי תּוֹרִישֵׁמוֹ יָדִי: נָשַׁפְתָּ בְרוּחֲךָ כִּסָּמוֹ יָם, צָלְלוּ כַּעוֹפֶרֶת בְּמַיִם אַדִּירִים: מִי כָמֹכָה בָּאֵלִם יְיָ, מִי כָּמֹכָה נֶאְדָּר בַּקֹּדֶשׁ, נוֹרָא תְהִלֹּת עֹשֵׂה פֶלֶא: נָטִיתָ יְמִינְךָ תִּבְלָעֵמוֹ אָרֶץ: נָחִיתָ בְחַסְדְּךָ עַם זוּ גָּאָלְתָּ, נֵהַלְתָּ בְעָזְּךָ אֶל נְוֵה קָדְשֶׁךָ: שָׁמְעוּ עַמִּים יִרְגָּזוּן, חִיל אָחַז יֹשְׁבֵי פְּלָשֶׁת: אָז נִבְהֲלוּ אַלּוּפֵי אֱדוֹם, אֵילֵי מוֹאָב יֹאחֲזֵמוֹ רָעַד נָמֹגוּ כֹּל יֹשְׁבֵי כְנָעַן: תִּפֹּל עֲלֵיהֶם אֵימָתָה וָפַחַד בִּגְדֹל זְרוֹעֲךָ יִדְּמוּ כָּאָבֶן: עַד יַעֲבֹר עַמְּךָ יְיָ, עַד יַעֲבֹר עַם זוּ קָנִיתָ: תְּבִאֵמוֹ וְתִטָּעֵמוֹ בְּהַר נַחֲלָתְךָ, מָכוֹן לְשִׁבְתְּךָ פָּעַלְתָּ יְיָ, מִקְּדָשׁ אֲדֹנָי כּוֹנְנוּ יָדֶיךָ: יְיָ | יִמְלֹךְ לְעֹלָם וָעֶד: יְיָ יִמְלֹךְ לְעֹלָם וָעֶד:

My favorite prayer is *Az Yashir Moshe* (The Song of The Sea) from the morning *Shaharit* service. This prayer is one of the earliest affirmations of faith in the Jewish tradition. It is believed to have been sung by the Israelites in praise and thanksgiving of God's deliverance of them from the bondage of slavery in Egypt.

I first became acquainted with the prayer while saying *Kaddish* for my parents. Each day, I looked forward to its haunting beauty. The rhythmic cadence and ancient melody soothed and calmed me through my journey of grief and acceptance of loss. It reminded me of how belief in God sustains us in times of crisis and how prayer can restore and renew our spirit.

The prayer is linked to Exodus and to Passover, my favorite holiday. Just as I experience a connection with all my Jewish ancestors through the rituals of the Passover Seder, *Az Yashir Moshe* reminds me of the richness of my Jewish heritage that brings me comfort, support, and guidance through all my life experiences.

Az Yashir Moshe (Exodus 15:1-18)

Rabbi Steven A. Schwarzman

This is the majestic Song at the Sea, the song of praise that Exodus itself tells us Moses and the children of Israel sang after crossing over safely, and of course Miriam and the women sang a similar or identical song as they danced with timbrels.

And yet, while this song is one of celebration, marking the miraculous delivery of the Israelites from the pursuing Egyptians…it has some very down-to-earth details.

I'm not actually thinking about the description of the Egyptian army and its horses and chariots falling into the sea. I'm thinking about signs in gift shops in modern Israel.

Like shops anywhere, the owners want to protect their investments in the fragile merchandise on their shelves. So they sometimes put up signs that say, *shavarta – kanita*, or "if you break it, it's yours."

The interesting word is *kanita* – you have acquired it. And it's interesting because it appears in this Biblical text, toward the end of the part that we read: *ad ya'avor amkha adonai; ad-ya'avor am-zu kanita* – until Your people cross over, God; until this people that You have acquired crosses over.

Like porcelain or other fragile items in a shop, we can easily be broken. But the One who created all chose to acquire us and help us across the Red Sea, and so we cannot be so easily broken after all. We are strong through God's strength.

Nishmat Kol Hai (on Shabbat)

Cantor Jack Chomsky

נִשְׁמַת כָּל חַי, תְּבָרֵךְ אֶת שִׁמְךָ יְיָ אֱלֹהֵינוּ. וְרוּחַ כָּל בָּשָׂר, תְּפָאֵר וּתְרוֹמֵם זִכְרְךָ מַלְכֵּנוּ תָּמִיד, מִן הָעוֹלָם וְעַד הָעוֹלָם אַתָּה אֵל. וּמִבַּלְעָדֶיךָ אֵין לָנוּ מֶלֶךְ גּוֹאֵל וּמוֹשִׁיעַ, פּוֹדֶה וּמַצִּיל וּמְפַרְנֵס וּמְרַחֵם, בְּכָל עֵת צָרָה וְצוּקָה. אֵין לָנוּ מֶלֶךְ אֶלָּא אָתָּה: אֱלֹהֵי הָרִאשׁוֹנִים וְהָאַחֲרוֹנִים, אֱלוֹהַּ כָּל בְּרִיּוֹת, אֲדוֹן כָּל תּוֹלָדוֹת, הַמְהֻלָּל בְּרֹב הַתִּשְׁבָּחוֹת, הַמְנַהֵג עוֹלָמוֹ בְּחֶסֶד, וּבְרִיּוֹתָיו בְּרַחֲמִים. וַיְיָ לֹא יָנוּם וְלֹא יִישָׁן, הַמְעוֹרֵר יְשֵׁנִים וְהַמֵּקִיץ נִרְדָּמִים, וְהַמֵּשִׂיחַ אִלְּמִים, וְהַמַּתִּיר אֲסוּרִים, וְהַסּוֹמֵךְ נוֹפְלִים, וְהַזּוֹקֵף כְּפוּפִים, לְךָ לְבַדְּךָ אֲנַחְנוּ מוֹדִים. אִלּוּ פִינוּ מָלֵא שִׁירָה כַּיָּם, וּלְשׁוֹנֵנוּ רִנָּה כַּהֲמוֹן גַּלָּיו, וְשִׂפְתוֹתֵינוּ שֶׁבַח כְּמֶרְחֲבֵי רָקִיעַ, וְעֵינֵינוּ מְאִירוֹת כַּשֶּׁמֶשׁ וְכַיָּרֵחַ, וְיָדֵינוּ פְרוּשׂוֹת כְּנִשְׁרֵי שָׁמָיִם, וְרַגְלֵינוּ קַלּוֹת כָּאַיָּלוֹת, אֵין אֲנַחְנוּ מַסְפִּיקִים, לְהוֹדוֹת לְךָ יְיָ אֱלֹהֵינוּ וֵאלֹהֵי אֲבוֹתֵינוּ, וּלְבָרֵךְ אֶת שִׁמְךָ עַל אַחַת מֵאֶלֶף אֶלֶף אַלְפֵי אֲלָפִים וְרִבֵּי רְבָבוֹת פְּעָמִים, הַטּוֹבוֹת שֶׁעָשִׂיתָ עִם אֲבוֹתֵינוּ וְעִמָּנוּ. מִמִּצְרַיִם גְּאַלְתָּנוּ יְיָ אֱלֹהֵינוּ, וּמִבֵּית עֲבָדִים פְּדִיתָנוּ, בְּרָעָב זַנְתָּנוּ, וּבְשָׂבָע כִּלְכַּלְתָּנוּ, מֵחֶרֶב הִצַּלְתָּנוּ, וּמִדֶּבֶר מִלַּטְתָּנוּ, וּמֵחֳלָיִם רָעִים וְנֶאֱמָנִים דִּלִּיתָנוּ: עַד הֵנָּה עֲזָרוּנוּ רַחֲמֶיךָ, וְלֹא עֲזָבוּנוּ חֲסָדֶיךָ, וְאַל תִּטְּשֵׁנוּ יְיָ אֱלֹהֵינוּ לָנֶצַח. עַל כֵּן אֵבָרִים שֶׁפִּלַּגְתָּ בָּנוּ, וְרוּחַ וּנְשָׁמָה שֶׁנָּפַחְתָּ בְּאַפֵּינוּ, וְלָשׁוֹן אֲשֶׁר שַׂמְתָּ בְּפִינוּ. הֵן הֵם יוֹדוּ וִיבָרְכוּ וִישַׁבְּחוּ וִיפָאֲרוּ וִירוֹמְמוּ וְיַעֲרִיצוּ וְיַקְדִּישׁוּ וְיַמְלִיכוּ אֶת שִׁמְךָ מַלְכֵּנוּ, כִּי כָל פֶּה לְךָ יוֹדֶה, וְכָל לָשׁוֹן לְךָ תִשָּׁבַע, וְכָל בֶּרֶךְ לְךָ תִכְרַע, וְכָל קוֹמָה לְפָנֶיךָ תִשְׁתַּחֲוֶה, וְכָל לְבָבוֹת יִירָאוּךָ, וְכָל קֶרֶב וּכְלָיוֹת יְזַמְּרוּ לִשְׁמֶךָ. כַּדָּבָר שֶׁכָּתוּב, כָּל עַצְמוֹתַי תֹּאמַרְנָה יְיָ מִי כָמוֹךָ. מַצִּיל עָנִי מֵחָזָק מִמֶּנּוּ, וְעָנִי וְאֶבְיוֹן מִגֹּזְלוֹ: מִי יִדְמֶה לָּךְ, וּמִי יִשְׁוֶה לָּךְ וּמִי יַעֲרָךְ לָךְ: הָאֵל הַגָּדוֹל הַגִּבּוֹר וְהַנּוֹרָא, אֵל עֶלְיוֹן קֹנֵה שָׁמַיִם וָאָרֶץ: נְהַלֶּלְךָ וּנְשַׁבֵּחֲךָ וּנְפָאֶרְךָ וּנְבָרֵךְ אֶת שֵׁם קָדְשֶׁךָ. כָּאָמוּר, לְדָוִד, בָּרְכִי נַפְשִׁי אֶת יְיָ, וְכָל קְרָבַי אֶת שֵׁם קָדְשׁוֹ:

A favorite personal prayer is *Nishmat Kol Hai*, which is recited on Shabbat morning just before the *hazzan* begins at *Shokhen Ad*. It has a number of features that make me smile and feel good, and I feel that it's unfortunate that so little attention is paid to it in *shul*: It's always a challenge to recite all its words in the time allotted to it – and of course many people are nowhere near *shul* at this point in the service.

What makes it great (among other things) is the physicality of it – and the lavish language of love and adoration. It goes through different parts of the body (mouth, tongue, lips, eyes, arms, legs) and describes them at ultra-peak performance, and says that this would represent not even one thousand-thousand-thousandth of the gratitude that we ought to feel to God – just for existence!

And I believe that the prayer has its math right – that our mere existence is a blessing that is profound beyond words, emotion, and our physical power – so how much more so for the rest of what we've got.

And what I've described is just one part of this prayer – about one-quarter of its amazing journey.

The recitation of *nishmat kol hai* (or in this case the *ilu finu malei* section of it) really prepares me spiritually and physically to approach the lectern at *shokhen ad* – but also prepares me personally to be a better husband, father, and person, appreciative of the blessings I receive from those around me – and can share with them.

That's a great prayer!

Nishmat Kol Hai (on Shabbat)

Barry Barnes

My favorite prayer is *Nishmat Kol Hai*. It speaks to the fact that the soul of every living thing should praise Hashem. No distinction is made between the people of Israel, the Jews, and the rest of the world. It speaks to the supremacy of Hashem in creating the entire world without distinction.

Coming as it does after the praises of the psalms that start the service, and after Moses' Song at the Sea, it sets a mood to prepare us for contemplating the role we have, and sets the stage for the structured prayers that follow. We recognize that each of us is miniscule compared to Hashem and the universe, yet it speaks to us of our singular value as human beings.

Linked to this is my favorite phrase, one by which I try to live my life. It comes near the end of the *Hallel*: *Zeh hayom asah Hashem, nagilah v'nismehah vo* – This is the day Hashem has made, let us rejoice and be glad on it.

As each year passes, it becomes clearer and clearer to me that we have to take each day, live it to the fullest, and be thankful for the blessing of living another day.

Ilu Finu (on Shabbat)

Hazzan Shoshana Brown

אִלּוּ פִינוּ מָלֵא שִׁירָה כַּיָּם, וּלְשׁוֹנֵנוּ רִנָּה כַּהֲמוֹן גַּלָּיו, וְשִׂפְתוֹתֵינוּ שֶׁבַח
כְּמֶרְחֲבֵי רָקִיעַ, וְעֵינֵינוּ מְאִירוֹת כַּשֶּׁמֶשׁ וְכַיָּרֵחַ, וְיָדֵינוּ פְרוּשׂוֹת כְּנִשְׁרֵי
שָׁמָיִם, וְרַגְלֵינוּ קַלּוֹת כָּאַיָּלוֹת, אֵין אֲנַחְנוּ מַסְפִּיקִים, לְהוֹדוֹת לְךָ יְיָ
אֱלֹהֵינוּ וֵאלֹהֵי אֲבוֹתֵינוּ, וּלְבָרֵךְ אֶת שְׁמֶךָ עַל אַחַת מֵאֶלֶף אֶלֶף אַלְפֵי
אֲלָפִים וְרִבֵּי רְבָבוֹת פְּעָמִים, הַטּוֹבוֹת שֶׁעָשִׂיתָ עִם אֲבוֹתֵינוּ וְעִמָּנוּ.

Ilu finu malei shirah ka-yam...This liturgical poem,
singing of the impossibility of being able to utter deep
enough, or "shining" enough praise to God for all the
myriads of kindnesses that God has done for us and
our ancestors, has been my favorite piece of liturgy
for many years...and it's not because of its literal
meaning.

Yes, God has done some great things for us and our
ancestors...but let's face it – there have been all too
many dark times when God has not come through,
and no miracles occurred to rescue us from death or
terrible suffering. It's because the *payetan* (liturgical
poet), in describing the kinds of praises that he would
like to be able to offer – praises filling our mouths as
the waves fill the sea; our tongues as expansive as the
very stretch of the blue sky above us; our eyes shining
like the sun and moon; our arms stretched out in
praise like the wings of the eagles of the heavens; our
feet dancing in praise like the light feet of the gazelle
– takes us on a virtual tour of the beauties of the
planet. How brilliant and majestic is God's dear
Creation and creatures!

I think of the so well-loved poem of Hannah Sennesh: *Eli, Eli, shelo yigamer l'olam...* - "My God, my God, I pray that these things never end: the sand and the sea, the rush of the waters, the crash of the heavens, the prayer of the human being."

When I sing *Ilu Finu*, I am not so much singing thanks for what God has done for me or my ancestors in history. I am singing thanks and praise for the sea, the sun, the moon, the sparkle of sunlight on the water, the leap of the gazelle and all the other graceful creatures that still dance upon the face of our planet...and like Hannah Sennesh, I am praying that they stay with us, keep leaping and dancing, shining and splashing – world without end.

I was sad for many years that no *shul* I'd ever been to had a special tune for this *piyyut*. It was *davened* over so speedily – as if the prayer-leader had never noticed how beautiful the words were (and if you don't get to the *shul* early enough, you'll miss it altogether!).

Then one Shabbat morning I was at Elat Chayyim, the Jewish Renewal Retreat Center – the old one, when it was still in the Catskills – and on this morning, we were *davening* inside, up at the center that was on the crest of the hill, with its big plate-glass windows that looked out across the valley and at the mountain ridge on the other side. It was common to see large birds like hawks soaring across the big open horizon there.

And I heard my dear musician-friend Pinchas Zohav sing out his own composition of *Ilu Finu*, while playing along on his guitar, and I began to sing along, and the tears started flowing fast...finally someone had composed a fitting tune for these beautiful words!

The whole *kahal* (congregation) slowed down and sang along, and at last the words were taken in, were noticed, got to shine as they should...at last the words filled our mouths as the waves fill the sea, and our eyes shone like the sun and moon, and we stretched out our arms and took flight with the hawk and the eagle, and women and men danced like gazelles! I will never forget that shining Shabbat morning, and will always be grateful to dear Pinchas who brought this *piyyut* to life! To this day in my work as a *hazzan*, I love to teach this tune in his name, and to share with others this ancient paean to the Creator and Creation.

Ilu Finu (on Shabbat)

Heather G. Stoltz

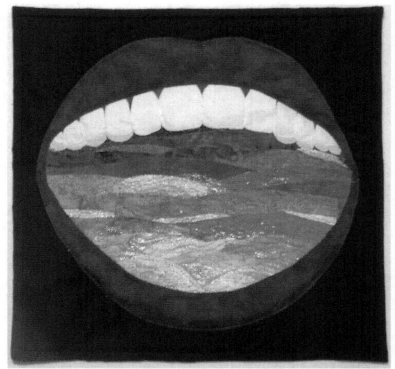

This quilt was inspired by the words *"Ilu finu maleh shirah kayam* – Could song fill our mouths as water fills the sea" which appear in the Shabbat and Festival liturgy. The text goes on to say "...could joy flood our tongue like countless waves ... never could we fully state our gratitude for one ten-thousandth of the lasting love which is Your precious blessing, dearest God, granted to our ancestors and to us." This quilt tries to capture the desire to offer thanks and praise that language is incapable of expressing. It is only through our limited human abilities of art, song, and references to the wonders of nature that we can try to communicate our thanks to the Creator of the universe.

The quilt is made from hand-painted and commercial fabrics, cellophane, and Angelina fibers. Musical notes and G clefs are quilted into the waves, which fill this mouth. In order to further involve song in the piece, a recording device, sewn into the bottom right corner of the quilt, plays a short clip of *Ilu Finu* by Miriam Margles, recorded by Kim and Reggie Harris and Rabbi Jonathan Kligler.

Yishtabah

Rabbi Steven A. Schwarzman

יִשְׁתַּבַּח שִׁמְךָ לָעַד מַלְכֵּנוּ, הָאֵל הַמֶּלֶךְ הַגָּדוֹל וְהַקָּדוֹשׁ בַּשָּׁמַיִם וּבָאָרֶץ. כִּי לְךָ נָאֶה, יְיָ אֱלֹהֵינוּ וֵאלֹהֵי אֲבוֹתֵינוּ: שִׁיר וּשְׁבָחָה, הַלֵּל וְזִמְרָה, עֹז וּמֶמְשָׁלָה, נֶצַח, גְּדֻלָּה וּגְבוּרָה, תְּהִלָּה וְתִפְאֶרֶת, קְדֻשָּׁה וּמַלְכוּת. בְּרָכוֹת וְהוֹדָאוֹת מֵעַתָּה וְעַד עוֹלָם. בָּרוּךְ אַתָּה יְיָ, אֵל מֶלֶךְ גָּדוֹל בַּתִּשְׁבָּחוֹת, אֵל הַהוֹדָאוֹת, אֲדוֹן הַנִּפְלָאוֹת, הַבּוֹחֵר בְּשִׁירֵי זִמְרָה, מֶלֶךְ, אֵל, חֵי הָעוֹלָמִים.

Pesukei Dezimrah, the Verses of Praise, conclude with *Yishtabah.* Depending on how fast we've been going, we've spent perhaps a half-hour singing praises to warm up our praying sensitivities. And we end this section of our prayers with – what else? – a recognition that we have barely scratched the surface.

We pray: *yishtabah shimkha la-ad malkeinu* – may your name, our King, be praised forever.

Not to worry – the service will not go on forever! But we recognize that if we could, we would do just that. Because it is fitting, we go on to say: *ki lekha naeh.* For You, it would be appropriate, to go on *mei-atah ve-ad olam* – from now until eternity.

Keep that in mind the next time you're tempted to look at your watch during the service!

Chapter 4
Shma and its Blessings

Probably every Jew knows the *Shma*. Central as *Shma* is, it, too, comes with a small package of blessings before and after it, building up to it and leading us gently back down from it partway, morning and evening, as we prepare for the *Amidah* that follows.

– *Rabbi Steven A. Schwarzman*

Hameir La'aretz

Rabbi Steven A. Schwarzman

הַמֵּאִיר לָאָרֶץ וְלַדָּרִים עָלֶיהָ בְּרַחֲמִים, וּבְטוּבוֹ מְחַדֵּשׁ בְּכָל יוֹם תָּמִיד
מַעֲשֵׂה בְרֵאשִׁית: מָה רַבּוּ מַעֲשֶׂיךָ יְיָ, כֻּלָּם בְּחָכְמָה עָשִׂיתָ, מָלְאָה
הָאָרֶץ קִנְיָנֶךָ: הַמֶּלֶךְ הַמְרוֹמָם לְבַדּוֹ מֵאָז. הַמְשֻׁבָּח וְהַמְפֹאָר
וְהַמִּתְנַשֵּׂא מִימוֹת עוֹלָם: אֱלֹהֵי עוֹלָם, בְּרַחֲמֶיךָ הָרַבִּים רַחֵם עָלֵינוּ,
אֲדוֹן עֻזֵּנוּ צוּר מִשְׂגַּבֵּנוּ, מָגֵן יִשְׁעֵנוּ מִשְׂגָּב בַּעֲדֵנוּ: אֵל בָּרוּךְ גְּדוֹל דֵּעָה.
הֵכִין וּפָעַל זָהֳרֵי חַמָּה. טוֹב יָצַר כָּבוֹד לִשְׁמוֹ. מְאוֹרוֹת נָתַן סְבִיבוֹת
עֻזּוֹ, פִּנּוֹת צְבָאָיו קְדוֹשִׁים, רוֹמְמֵי שַׁדַּי. תָּמִיד מְסַפְּרִים, כְּבוֹד אֵל
וּקְדֻשָּׁתוֹ: תִּתְבָּרַךְ יְיָ אֱלֹהֵינוּ עַל שֶׁבַח מַעֲשֵׂה יָדֶיךָ. וְעַל מְאוֹרֵי אוֹר
שֶׁעָשִׂיתָ יְפָאֲרוּךָ סֶּלָה.

Right after *Barkhu*, we retake our seats for the first of
the blessings that come before *Shma*. And we bless
God as the one who mercifully provides light to the
Earth and to its inhabitants – literally, those who
dwell on it. (The same word is used for tenants,
people who just happen to live in a place that looks
like it belongs to them, but really belongs to someone
else.)

Really? Can you imagine that God might create a
world and then forget, as it were, to turn on the
lights?

I think the key is "mercifully" – a word that, in
Hebrew, comes at the end of the phrase. The mercy
that God shows in this act is to us, those who dwell
on Earth. And the prayer goes on to explain: in
goodness, God renews the work of creation every
single day.

Creation, you see, didn't just happen long ago. It still
happens, every day. It's an ongoing project. Not

because we deserve it – this is the "mercifully" part – but because this is how God, our landlord, the owner of our residence, is. In fact, we go on to ask in this prayer explicitly for God, who is eternal, to have mercy on us. We don't say here how temporal we are, but we are thinking it.

Thank you, God, for keeping the lights on for us.

L'El Barukh Ne'imot Yiteinu

Rabbi Samuel Barth

לְאֵל בָּרוּךְ נְעִימוֹת יִתֵּנוּ. לְמֶלֶךְ אֵל חַי וְקַיָּם זְמִרוֹת יֹאמֵרוּ וְתִשְׁבָּחוֹת יַשְׁמִיעוּ. כִּי הוּא לְבַדּוֹ פּוֹעֵל גְּבוּרוֹת, עֹשֶׂה חֲדָשׁוֹת, בַּעַל מִלְחָמוֹת, זוֹרֵעַ צְדָקוֹת, מַצְמִיחַ יְשׁוּעוֹת, בּוֹרֵא רְפוּאוֹת, נוֹרָא תְהִלּוֹת, אֲדוֹן הַנִּפְלָאוֹת. הַמְחַדֵּשׁ בְּטוּבוֹ בְּכָל יוֹם תָּמִיד מַעֲשֵׂה בְרֵאשִׁית. כָּאָמוּר לְעֹשֵׂה אוֹרִים גְּדֹלִים, כִּי לְעוֹלָם חַסְדּוֹ : אוֹר חָדָשׁ עַל צִיּוֹן תָּאִיר וְנִזְכֶּה כֻלָּנוּ מְהֵרָה לְאוֹרוֹ : בָּרוּךְ אַתָּה יְיָ יוֹצֵר הַמְּאוֹרוֹת :

Or hadash al Tsiyon ta'ir, venizkeh khulanu m'heirah le'oro – Cause a new light to shine on Zion, and may we all quickly have the privilege to benefit from its radiance.

Each morning, before reciting the *Shma*, there is a blessing that opens with a quote from Isaiah praising God, "who forms light and creates darkness," and looks back to the first great act of Creation—the creation of light and the establishment of cycles of light and darkness, designated as day and night.

Many commentators have wondered about the *or hadash* introduced at the very end of this blessing. What does the phrase mean—is this new light to be somehow different? Will the laws of physics be abrogated, upsetting the natural order of the universe?

An alternate approach is to understand this as an entirely heavenly light, associated with the end of time, the messianic era. We recall the enigmatic prophetic metaphor, "In those days the sun will not be your light by day, nor the moon at night, but God will be your Eternal illumination (Isa. 60:19)." This certainly evokes a supernal, God-centered "light," and many commentators suggest that these words represent a yearning for messianic redemption. Some authorities, including Saadia Gaon (10th century), judged this messianic reference to be so anomalous that it should be removed entirely.

Aryeh Leib Gordon (19th-century Vilna) finds a middle pathway in his *Tikkun Tefillah* commentary. After quoting Proverbs 6:23 — "For commandment is a lamp and the Torah is light." — he observes, "There is yet a light greater and more exalted than the sun— and this (light) is the Torah!" Gordon's synthetic approach allows us to retain the idea of a spiritual light without messianic overtones.

During Hanukkah, we encounter lights each day. These lights embody holiness. Perhaps they inspire us to draw close to the Torah that is abidingly close to us, and to dream of the ethereal light in which all things will be seen with a greater and deeper clarity.

L'El Barukh Ne'imot Yiteinu

Rabbi Steven A. Schwarzman

Toward the end of the first blessing before *Shma* comes a series of descriptions of God based on what we observe of God's actions in this world. We, or perhaps the angels mentioned earlier in the prayer, offer songs to God, who is alive, who alone does mighty deeds, creates new things, owns wars, sows righteousnesses (yes, in the plural), plants salvations, creates healings, is awed in praises, master of wonders.

We're not surprised that God does mighty deeds or creates new things. And I don't profess to understand fully what it means that God owns wars. But whatever that is, it is followed by no less than three seemingly simple yet wonderful characteristics of God: God sows righteousnesses. Not one, but many. God, as it were, goes around planting righteousness here, righteousness there. It may take a while for that righteousness to sprout, and maybe – even with God as the sower – maybe not all of them will take root if the local conditions are not conducive. But over time, we understand, these plantings will bear more and more fruit, and spread.

And it is not only righteousnesses that God plants; God also plants salvations – again, in the plural. Not just one. Multiple salvations. Enough salvations for whatever we need to be saved from. Enough salvations to go around for everybody.

And healings. These are not planted by God, but created by God, the same way that the world itself is created, using the same verb. God creates healings, multiple healings. Healings of spirit, healings of body. Healings of hearts, healings of mind. Healings of our ancestors, healings of us today.

Ahavah Rabbah

Rabbi Steven A. Schwarzman

אַהֲבָה רַבָּה אֲהַבְתָּנוּ, יְיָ אֱלֹהֵינוּ, חֶמְלָה גְדוֹלָה וִיתֵרָה חָמַלְתָּ עָלֵינוּ. אָבִינוּ מַלְכֵּנוּ, בַּעֲבוּר אֲבוֹתֵינוּ שֶׁבָּטְחוּ בְךָ, וַתְּלַמְּדֵם חֻקֵּי חַיִּים, כֵּן תְּחָנֵּנוּ וּתְלַמְּדֵנוּ. אָבִינוּ, הָאָב הָרַחֲמָן, הַמְרַחֵם, רַחֵם עָלֵינוּ, וְתֵן בְּלִבֵּנוּ לְהָבִין וּלְהַשְׂכִּיל, לִשְׁמֹעַ, לִלְמֹד וּלְלַמֵּד, לִשְׁמֹר וְלַעֲשׂוֹת וּלְקַיֵּם אֶת כָּל דִּבְרֵי תַלְמוּד תּוֹרָתֶךָ בְּאַהֲבָה. וְהָאֵר עֵינֵינוּ בְּתוֹרָתֶךָ, וְדַבֵּק לִבֵּנוּ בְּמִצְוֹתֶיךָ, וְיַחֵד לְבָבֵנוּ לְאַהֲבָה וּלְיִרְאָה אֶת שְׁמֶךָ, וְלֹא נֵבוֹשׁ לְעוֹלָם וָעֶד: כִּי בְשֵׁם קָדְשְׁךָ הַגָּדוֹל וְהַנּוֹרָא בָּטָחְנוּ, נָגִילָה וְנִשְׂמְחָה בִּישׁוּעָתֶךָ. וַהֲבִיאֵנוּ לְשָׁלוֹם מֵאַרְבַּע כַּנְפוֹת הָאָרֶץ, וְתוֹלִכֵנוּ קוֹמְמִיּוּת לְאַרְצֵנוּ, כִּי אֵל פּוֹעֵל יְשׁוּעוֹת אָתָּה, וּבָנוּ בָחַרְתָּ מִכָּל עַם וְלָשׁוֹן. וְקֵרַבְתָּנוּ לְשִׁמְךָ הַגָּדוֹל סֶלָה בֶּאֱמֶת לְהוֹדוֹת לְךָ וּלְיַחֶדְךָ בְּאַהֲבָה. בָּרוּךְ אַתָּה יְיָ, הַבּוֹחֵר בְּעַמּוֹ יִשְׂרָאֵל בְּאַהֲבָה.

God loves us. I know, that sounds obvious, perhaps, but it's a good thing to keep in mind when we fall out of love with ourselves. And it doesn't have to do with how great we might or might not be, because it's really about God's compassion – and that doesn't depend on human behavior.

Still, we remind God – or perhaps ourselves – that our ancestors trusted in God, who taught them laws for living that we, too, want to learn. We ask God to let our hearts and minds understand and learn, and eventually teach, Torah with love. We ask God to brighten our eyes with Torah and to cleave our hearts and minds to the commandments like glue, to take our usually fragmented hearts and minds and unify them in love and awe of God's name, so that we need never feel shame.

Focusing on the right things in life is truly what keeps us from having to feel shame. *Halakhah* (Jewish law) instructs us, when we visit someone seriously ill, to ask them if they have their affairs in order. Have they lent something to someone? Have they borrowed something from someone? We help them straighten out their affairs so that they need not be afraid.

Afraid? Why would a gravely ill person be afraid about having borrowed the neighbor's lawnmower?

I think the *halakhah* is incredibly perceptive here. When we have unfinished business, the codes go on to say, we are afraid of death. And it's not really about the mundane things we might have borrowed or lent out. It's really about the issues we all care about: have we established or repaired our relationships with our loved ones? Have we spent the time we needed to in learning Torah, both for its own sake and so that we could do a decent job in living the commandments? Have we lived the way we really want to?

Of course, the idea behind the questions we ask gently, appropriately, sensitively is that the person we are visiting can work to fix those errors if they recover, and perhaps we can help them fix them now just in case.

So, too, when we are healthy. Or perhaps all the more so when we are healthy. If we sincerely ask God to defragment the hard drives of our hearts and brains, and if we do our own part to focus on the things and people that really count, then we really don't have much, or indeed anything, to fear.

We can, as the prayer goes on to say, rejoice in God's salvation. And just as we ask for God's help to reunite our thoughts and feelings, we ask also for God's help in reuniting the Jewish people in our land from the four corners of the earth. It's the custom when we say these words to gather the four *tzitziyot*, the four fringed threads of our *tallit*, and hold them together – because Jewish unity is not something that we expect God to impose on us from above. It's something that we have to actively build as well.

There are various opinions as to just how long one should keep these fringes together. In my own practice, I hold them until the last opinion says it's time to let them go. Unity is precious.

Shma

Keith Manaker

שְׁמַע יִשְׂרָאֵל, יְיָ אֱלֹהֵינוּ, יְיָ אֶחָד :

It is an almost impossible task to settle on a favorite Jewish prayer or to say which prayer I connect with most. It is like being asked to choose a favorite song, a favorite book, or a favorite work of art. So much of connecting with prayer has to do with my personal mood on a particular day, or events going on in my life. However, I believe that I can narrow down my list of most meaningful personal prayers to three. Of these three, there is really only one that truly sums up the purpose of life for me and helps me remember why I am here.

The *Shma* has been a very meaningful prayer for me throughout my adult Jewish life. Prior to coming back around to Judaism, I was searching for a spiritual connection. I especially enjoyed reading about Buddhist philosophy, and trying to comprehend the concept of "oneness", the interconnectedness of the universe, the common energy that runs through everything.

One day, I read a book called *The Jew in the Lotus*. In this book, a rabbi points out to the Dalai Lama that the *Shma* says that "God is One." Before reading *The Jew in the Lotus*, this line from the *Shma* had always meant to me that we can only have one God and that we cannot worship any other gods. It still means that to me, but now this line means much more.

When I say the *Shma*, it is a daily recognition that our God is not a separate entity. It's not that God is one and I am one. God is one and that oneness runs through everything, including me. We are all one with the Creator and with creation. Trying to comprehend the concept of "oneness" is a meditative, peaceful, and meaningful experience for me, because it connects me with my Creator.

Another prayer that has always been very meaningful to me is a line from *Hallel*. It states, "This is the day Hashem has made; let us rejoice and be glad on it." I believe that this single line may be the forefather of the concept of "trying to look on the bright side." It tells me that, no matter what is going on in my life, it is meant to be. The Creator made it that way. Surely, there is something about it that I can rejoice and be glad about.

While the line from *Hallel* and the *Shma* are very important and meaningful prayers for me, the line that sums it all up is the one that states, "We have not come into being to hate and destroy; we have come into being to praise, to labor, and to love." When I wonder why I am here or what is my purpose, this prayer gives me the answer. I am here to praise, to labor and to love. If I do nothing more with my life, I will leave that which is most important when I die. I will leave a good name and a memory that will be for a blessing.

Shma

Linda Friedman

When I pray the *Shma*, I am of course affirming my faith in God. But it means something more to me, since I am a person living alone, with my family living in different places.

I know God is one and pray that, wherever my loved ones are, He will watch over them. I literally think of each one to include them in my prayer. I have to rely on God to do what I can't – safeguard my family.

V'ahavta

Rabbi Samuel Barth

וְאָהַבְתָּ אֵת יְיָ אֱלֹהֶיךָ, בְּכָל-לְבָבְךָ, וּבְכָל-נַפְשְׁךָ, וּבְכָל-מְאֹדֶךָ. וְהָיוּ הַדְּבָרִים הָאֵלֶּה, אֲשֶׁר אָנֹכִי מְצַוְּךָ הַיּוֹם, עַל-לְבָבֶךָ: וְשִׁנַּנְתָּם לְבָנֶיךָ, וְדִבַּרְתָּ בָּם בְּשִׁבְתְּךָ בְּבֵיתֶךָ, וּבְלֶכְתְּךָ בַדֶּרֶךְ וּבְשָׁכְבְּךָ, וּבְקוּמֶךָ. וּקְשַׁרְתָּם לְאוֹת עַל-יָדֶךָ, וְהָיוּ לְטֹטָפֹת בֵּין עֵינֶיךָ, וּכְתַבְתָּם עַל מְזֻזֹת בֵּיתֶךָ וּבִשְׁעָרֶיךָ:

The first paragraph of the *Shma* invites us to affirm the unity of God, and then engages the topic of love, the love from a person to God: "*v'ahavta et Adonai Elohekha*" (You shall love Adonai your God). Several important questions present themselves. First, is the phrase "you shall love" to be understood as an imperative? The grammar supports such a construction, leading us to wonder how love can be commanded. Commands can be given to bring specified sacrifices, to eat *matzah* on *Pesah*, and to show deference to the old, but how can we be commanded to love? Some commentators avoid the dilemma by suggesting the meaning is that we are to behave in a way that would express our love for God, but this avoids the deeper question about how and why this love for God is born in our hearts and minds.

My friend Rabbi Leila Gal Berner suggests that the text can reasonably be read to suggest an element of Divine yearning. "Oh . . . if only you would love your God with all your heart, soul and might!" This is consistent with the Talmudic teaching, *rahaman liba ba'ei* (the All-Merciful desires [only] the human heart).

Reading in this way, the *Shma* invites us twice daily to offer the one thing that God cannot command—because it is impossible: human love.

In the evening and morning liturgy, the *Shma* is preceded by a paragraph that speaks of God's love for the Jewish People: in the evening, we find *"Ahavat olam beyt Yisrael ahavta"* (With eternal love have You loved Your people Israel); and in the morning, *"Ahavah rabah ahavtanu"* (With great love have You loved us). In each case, the text speaks of the Torah as the visible sign of God's love. It is given to us as a gift, and in that gift of love, in the text of the *Shma*, is the command/yearning for that love to be returned.

The liturgical texts offer us a pathway. The (evening) text of *Ahavat olam* states *"uv'Torato neh'geh yomam valaila"* (In his/His Torah we will meditate day and night). The words are ambiguous as to whether the Torah is "His" (God's) or "his" (the person praying). Rashi, commenting on the source of this phrase in Psalm 2, suggests a process: at first, the Torah belongs to God, but after a person learns and studies it, then that person becomes a partner with God for those words of Torah. Perhaps we can discern in this expression of mutuality about Torah a path to a relationship of growing love between each person and God. Love of God can arise in our hearts as we feel and perceive more and more that we are loved by God, always.

V'ahavta

Herb Daroff

The first paragraph after the *Shma* continues the lesson. But, I have always seen these words as poetry and not just taken literally.

Poetically, we bind the words of the *Shma* on our hand so that our actions are in line with God's teachings of right and wrong. Having these words be a reminder above our eyes is to help us be sure that our thoughts are Godly as well as our deeds. This is true with or without the literal interpretation of benching *tefillin*.

Inscribing God's oneness upon the doorposts of our homes as well as our gates reminds us to follow God's teachings not only at home or only at *shul*, but also after we leave those confines. Praying a few times a year, or every week, or every day does nothing for us if we then go out and cheat our employees or customers. That's not Godly. Giving lip service to loving our spouses and children morning and night, but then being unfaithful to them, is not Godly, either.

I believe that we are, by nature, uncivilized, prone to be unfaithful, prone to take advantage of those in weaker positions. I think that's part of survival of the fittest. However, being one with God and following teachings of the Torah brings us civility, a moral compass to follow day and night, at home or away.

I love the Rogers and Hammerstein lyric from *South Pacific*, "You've got to be carefully taught":

> *You've got to be taught to hate and fear,*
> *You've got to be taught from year to year,*
> *It's got to be drummed in your dear little ear,*
> *You've got to be carefully taught.*
>
> *You've got to be taught to be afraid*
> *Of people whose eyes are oddly made,*
> *And people whose skin is a diff'rent shade,*
> *You've got to be carefully taught.*
>
> *You've got to be taught before it's too late,*
> *Before you are six or seven or eight,*
> *To hate all the people your relatives hate,*
> *You've got to be carefully taught!*

but I'm not so sure they are right. Without God as our guide, we repeat the wrong behavior of those around us. Only with the lessons of Torah do we avoid the temptations and live by an ethical code. That is the burden of being God's Chosen People. It's not a privilege. It's an obligation to continue to show the world that even in the toughest times, we love our neighbors as much as we love ourselves.

Chapter 5
Amidah

In rabbinic parlance, what today we usually call the *Amidah* (because it is recited while standing), or *Shmoneh Esrei* (for the 18, later 19 benedictions in it) was originally called *Tefillah – the* prayer. It is the core of Jewish prayer. The three benedictions at the beginning and the three at the end are essentially the same in every *Amidah*; what changes are the benedictions in the middle.

On weekdays, there is a series of benedictions that include requests and petitions – not for ourselves, but for our people. On Shabbat and festivals, those benedictions are replaced by one shorter benediction focused on the theme of the day.

– Rabbi Steven A. Schwarzman

Amidah or Shemoneh Esrai?

David Sefton

Even though the Amidah is quite well organized, its title is a loaded discrepancy. The Amidah is also known as the *Shmoneh Esrai* (The 18); however, there are 19 prayers since the prayer that deals with slanderers was added. No one bothered to update the name.

This inconsistency between the number of prayers within the Amidah and its title tells me that there is nothing in Judaism that cannot be questioned. It permits me to be comfortable in my observance of Judaism and yet be skeptical at the same time.

Mehayeh Hameitim

Rabbi Steven A. Schwarzman

אַתָּה גִבּוֹר לְעוֹלָם אֲדֹנָי, מְחַיֵּה מֵתִים אַתָּה, רַב לְהוֹשִׁיעַ:

בחורף: מַשִּׁיב הָרוּחַ וּמוֹרִיד הַגָּשֶׁם:

מְכַלְכֵּל חַיִּים בְּחֶסֶד, מְחַיֵּה מֵתִים בְּרַחֲמִים רַבִּים, סוֹמֵךְ נוֹפְלִים, וְרוֹפֵא חוֹלִים, וּמַתִּיר אֲסוּרִים, וּמְקַיֵּם אֱמוּנָתוֹ לִישֵׁנֵי עָפָר, מִי כָמוֹךָ בַּעַל גְּבוּרוֹת וּמִי דּוֹמֶה לָּךְ, מֶלֶךְ מֵמִית וּמְחַיֶּה וּמַצְמִיחַ יְשׁוּעָה:

בעשי״ת: מִי כָמוֹךָ אַב הָרַחֲמִים, זוֹכֵר יְצוּרָיו לְחַיִּים בְּרַחֲמִים:

וְנֶאֱמָן אַתָּה לְהַחֲיוֹת מֵתִים. בָּרוּךְ אַתָּה יְיָ, מְחַיֵּה הַמֵּתִים:

Jews today are sometimes astonished to hear that Judaism believes quite strongly in resurrection of the dead. "Isn't that a Christian belief?" they ask. And I tell them that it is actually very much a Jewish belief, one that predates Christianity – indeed, while I claim no expertise in the history of Christian beliefs, it seems clear that the Christian belief in the resurrection of one particular Jew could not have come about without a prior belief among all Jews that resurrection would one day occur for everyone.

Well, not quite all Jews. The rabbis were quite adamant that Jews who did not believe in *tehiyat hameitim*, resurrection of the dead, were heretics. When warnings are issued with such strong language, this usually means that, while most people follow the norm, at least a few are not on board.

But for the last 2,000 years or so, Jews have very much believed that God will resurrect the dead as part of the final redemption. It's not an easy task, though, which is why our mention of this in the *Amidah* is located in the opening *gevurot* section, where we speak of God's might. "Your might is forever, Lord. You resurrect the dead, master of salvation." And then we go on to note how God grants life in the first place, again mentioning how God can then resurrect the dead in great mercy, support the falling, heal the sick, release the captive, and – yet again! – keep faith with those who sleep in the dust. And the blessing concludes with *three* more mentions of God's resurrection of the dead.

I think it should come as little surprise that we emphasize *tehiyat hameitim* so much. Yes, we need and pray for God's help during our lives. But even those of us most focused on this world must recognize that our lives here are short and of relatively small significance when compared to life in the next world – or to translate *olam haba* a little more closely, the world that is coming.

If you are thinking that all religions tackle this question of what happens after we die, you are right. But Judaism insists that it is within God's power to bring us back to life and redeem us, like the dry bones in Ezekiel's vision that come back to life.

I once visited an older woman who was terribly afraid of dying. She had lost some of her faculties, but her fear of dying was more than evident. She was sobbing when I entered her room.

I asked her what she thought would happen after she died. She said she didn't know, and she asked me the same question. So I told her about this very traditional Jewish belief, that death is not the end of our souls' existence, and that one day our souls and bodies will be reunited (and that our bodies will be healed). I told her that she would be reunited with her parents and her late husband.

Suddenly she looked at me with total clarity in her eyes. "Do you really believe that?" she asked. I told her that I did. And she was comforted.

So was I. So am I.

Atah Kadosh

Heather G. Stoltz

אַתָּה קָדוֹשׁ וְשִׁמְךָ קָדוֹשׁ וּקְדוֹשִׁים בְּכָל יוֹם יְהַלְלוּךָ, סֶלָה. בָּרוּךְ אַתָּה יְיָ,
הָאֵל הַקָּדוֹשׁ (בעשי"ת: הַמֶּלֶךְ הַקָּדוֹשׁ).

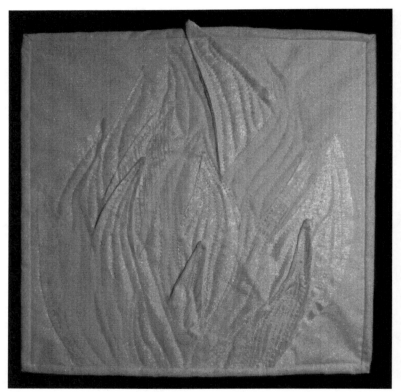

This piece is part of a series on the blessings of the weekday *Amidah* prayer. Through this blessing, which is recited every day, we acknowledge God's holiness.

This piece depicts a white flame, evoking the burning bush while maintaining a sense of purity. A longer version of this blessing is recited when ten or more people pray together; thus, the flames also represent the individuals who come together to praise God.

Kedushah

Linda Friedman

נְקַדֵּשׁ אֶת שִׁמְךָ בָּעוֹלָם, כְּשֵׁם שֶׁמַּקְדִּישִׁים אוֹתוֹ בִּשְׁמֵי מָרוֹם, כַּכָּתוּב
עַל יַד נְבִיאֶךָ, וְקָרָא זֶה אֶל זֶה וְאָמַר:

קָדוֹשׁ, קָדוֹשׁ, קָדוֹשׁ, יְיָ צְבָאוֹת, מְלֹא כָל הָאָרֶץ כְּבוֹדוֹ.

לְעֻמָּתָם בָּרוּךְ יֹאמֵרוּ:

בָּרוּךְ כְּבוֹד יְיָ מִמְּקוֹמוֹ.

וּבְדִבְרֵי קָדְשְׁךָ כָּתוּב לֵאמֹר:

יִמְלֹךְ יְיָ לְעוֹלָם, אֱלֹהַיִךְ צִיּוֹן, לְדֹר וָדֹר, הַלְלוּיָהּ.

שׁ״ץ: לְדוֹר וָדוֹר נַגִּיד גָּדְלֶךָ, וּלְנֵצַח נְצָחִים קְדֻשָּׁתְךָ נַקְדִּישׁ, וְשִׁבְחֲךָ,
אֱלֹהֵינוּ, מִפִּינוּ לֹא יָמוּשׁ לְעוֹלָם וָעֶד, כִּי אֵל מֶלֶךְ גָּדוֹל וְקָדוֹשׁ אָתָּה.
בָּרוּךְ אַתָּה יְיָ, הָאֵל הַקָּדוֹשׁ (בעשי״ת: הַמֶּלֶךְ הַקָּדוֹשׁ).

When I sing this prayer, I think of my children and
grandchildren. I am grateful that my children have
chosen Jewish mates who share in making Jewish
homes, and (in whatever form they have chosen)
continue to celebrate *Shabbat* and *Yom Tovim* with
their families.

I pray that my grandchildren will continue our
traditions, and "throughout all generations we will
declare Your greatness... and Your holiness."

Hashiveinu

Heather G. Stoltz

הֲשִׁיבֵנוּ אָבִינוּ לְתוֹרָתֶךָ, וְקָרְבֵנוּ מַלְכֵּנוּ לַעֲבוֹדָתֶךָ, וְהַחֲזִירֵנוּ בִּתְשׁוּבָה
שְׁלֵמָה לְפָנֶיךָ. בָּרוּךְ אַתָּה יְיָ, הָרוֹצֶה בִּתְשׁוּבָה.

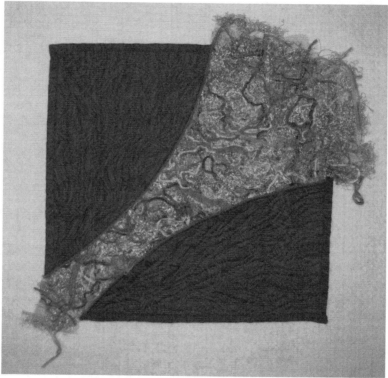

This piece is part of a series on the blessings of the weekday *Amidah* prayer. Through this blessing, which is recited every day, we ask God to lead us back to the right path.

In this piece, an open zipper represents this opening of the self as we show both God and ourselves the messy inside of our lives that we otherwise try to keep covered and under control.

Selah Lanu

Heather G. Stoltz

סְלַח לָנוּ, אָבִינוּ, כִּי חָטָאנוּ, מְחַל לָנוּ, מַלְכֵּנוּ כִּי פָשָׁעְנוּ, כִּי מוֹחֵל
וְסוֹלֵחַ אָתָּה. בָּרוּךְ אַתָּה יְיָ, חַנּוּן הַמַּרְבֶּה לִסְלֹחַ.

This piece is part of a series on the blessings of the weekday *Amidah* prayer. Through this blessing, which is recited every day, we admit to God that we have done wrong and ask for God's forgiveness.

In this piece, a closed zipper shows that God is forgiving, but the threads hanging out of the bottom remind us that we always live with the consequences of our actions.

Refa'enu

Rabbi Steven A. Schwarzman

רְפָאֵנוּ, יְיָ, וְנֵרָפֵא, הוֹשִׁיעֵנוּ וְנִוָּשֵׁעָה, כִּי תְהִלָּתֵנוּ אָתָּה, וְהַעֲלֵה רְפוּאָה
שְׁלֵמָה לְכָל מַכּוֹתֵינוּ. כִּי אֵל מֶלֶךְ רוֹפֵא נֶאֱמָן וְרַחֲמָן אָתָּה. בָּרוּךְ אַתָּה
יְיָ, רוֹפֵא חוֹלֵי עמוֹ יִשְׂרָאֵל.

In this prayer for healing, we are encouraged to
include a personal prayer for our own loved ones
who are not well. It doesn't require a *minyan*; it isn't
voiced out loud. It's a personal prayer that asks God
to send healing of body and of spirit to someone in
particular who needs it.

That phrase, healing of body and of spirit, which
seems to work better in that order in English, is
actually reversed in the Hebrew text of the prayer.
First we ask for *refuat hanefesh*, healing of the spirit,
and then we ask for *refuat haguf*, healing of the body.

Perhaps this is because healing of the spirit can help
with healing of the body. In some cases, I'm sure this
is so.

And in some cases, healing of the body is not
possible. Even then, it's still possible, and enormously
helpful, to ask for God's healing of the spirit, both of
the sick person we have in mind and of all those
taking care of that person. When a loved one is
seriously ill, unhealthy dynamics that usually reside
more or less quietly under the surface can come to the
fore as all involved consider the gravity of the
situation.

Healing of the spirit can help someone seriously ill be at peace, and it can help their loved ones be at peace, too.

Refa'enu

Rabbi Samuel Barth

In addition to the well-known *Mi Sheberakh* prayer for healing recited (or sung, in modern versions) during the *Shabbat* Torah Service, our liturgy engages with the theme of healing in the weekday *Amidah*, in the blessing that begins, *"Refa'einu Adonai veneirafei, hoshi'einu venivashe'a"* (Heal us, Adonai, and we shall be healed, save us and we shall be saved). The blessing continues, asking for complete healing (*refuah shleymah*) for all among the People of Israel who are unwell.

The blessing's opening words are perhaps the most intriguing and challenging, for they are quoted directly from Jeremiah (changed only by transforming the first person singular into the plural—"I" becomes "we"). However, the context of Jeremiah's words suggests that a more complex process is at work. In Jeremiah 17:13–15, we read:

> *Adonai, the hope of Israel, all who forsake You will be put to shame. Those who turn away on earth will be written down, because they have forsaken the fountain of living water, even Adonai. Heal me, Adonai, and I will be healed; Save me and I will be saved, for You are my praise. Look, they keep saying to me, "Where is the word of Adonai? Let it come now!"*

Now, it is certainly the case that Jeremiah invokes the concept of healing, and that the Hebrew word used is from the root that is now the basis of conventional medical healing: a physician in Hebrew is, of course, *rofeh*. However, Jeremiah does not seem to be asking to be healed from any medical condition—"healing" is, in this passionate request, set in poetic parallel to "salvation," and Jeremiah is seeking an end to spiritual anguish rather than a cure for the flu.

Perhaps this is the basis of the well-known and widespread phrase that appears in the *mi sheberakh* formula, *"refuat hanefesh urefuat haguf"* (healing of body and healing of soul). By invoking this text from Jeremiah, we assert and affirm the intrinsic connection between bodily and spiritual healing. We do not, of course, in any way discount the profound and critically important works of skilled physicians in diagnosis and medical care, but we acknowledge that the body does not exist alone and that the soul is intimately linked with it—the soul is always engaged in the process of healing and is sometimes the principal player.

We wonder always what response Jeremiah found to his inner anguish. Certainly it was not penicillin—but it may have been the healing waters of Torah.

Barekh Aleinu

Rabbi Steven A. Schwarzman

בָּרֵךְ עָלֵינוּ, יְיָ אֱלֹהֵינוּ, אֶת הַשָּׁנָה הַזֹּאת וְאֶת כָּל מִינֵי תְבוּאָתָהּ
לְטוֹבָה,

(בַּקַּיִץ) וְתֵן בְּרָכָה (בַּחֹרֶף) וְתֵן טַל וּמָטָר לִבְרָכָה

עַל פְּנֵי הָאֲדָמָה, וְשַׂבְּעֵנוּ מִטּוּבֶךָ, וּבָרֵךְ שְׁנָתֵנוּ כַּשָּׁנִים הַטּוֹבוֹת. בָּרוּךְ
אַתָּה יְיָ, מְבָרֵךְ הַשָּׁנִים.

We ask God to bless this year, and the blessing we are
talking about is rain so that crops can grow. One of
the questions I have been asked several times as a
rabbi is why one line in this prayer changes not based
on the Jewish calendar but the Gregorian one.

The answer, interestingly enough, is that it's actually
based on the Julian calendar, the one that preceded
the Gregorian one. The date – currently around
December 4 – is supposed to be 60 days after the
autumn equinox. Because this linkage was created
when the Jewish calendar was fixed, replacing the
ancient system of witnesses testifying about seeing
the new moon, the calendar in use at the time was the
Julian one.

But that's not the really interesting thing about this
prayer. The really cool thing is that we say this every
weekday of the year...including on the eve of Rosh
Hashanah, late in the afternoon of the last day of the
year.

Think about it: with only a few minutes left in the old
year, we ask God to make this year a good one. Next

year, which on that particular day will begin in just a few minutes, will have its own blessings. But meantime, we are still concerned about *this* year, a year that has only minutes left in it.

This is a powerful lesson in making time count. The next time you find yourself with an hour to "kill," remember this prayer. Don't kill that hour; make it an hour that brings a little more blessing into your life and the lives of those around you.

Al Hatzadikim

Rabbi Steven A. Schwarzman

עַל הַצַּדִּיקִים וְעַל הַחֲסִידִים וְעַל זִקְנֵי עַמְּךָ בֵּית יִשְׂרָאֵל, וְעַל פְּלֵיטַת
סוֹפְרֵיהֶם, וְעַל גֵּרֵי הַצֶּדֶק וְעָלֵינוּ, יֶהֱמוּ נָא רַחֲמֶיךָ, יְיָ אֱלֹהֵינוּ, וְתֵן
שָׂכָר טוֹב לְכָל הַבּוֹטְחִים בְּשִׁמְךָ בֶּאֱמֶת, וְשִׂים חֶלְקֵנוּ עִמָּהֶם לְעוֹלָם,
וְלֹא נֵבוֹשׁ כִּי בְךָ בָּטָחְנוּ. בָּרוּךְ אַתָּה יְיָ, מִשְׁעָן וּמִבְטָח לַצַּדִּיקִים.

> *On the righteous and the pious, on the elders of*
> *your people the House of Israel and on the remnant*
> *of their scholars, on true proselytes and on us, may*
> *your mercies, God, be stirred.*

> *Give a good reward to all who trust in your name in*
> *truth, and place our lot with them. May we never be*
> *ashamed, because in You we have trusted.*

We may or may not have much merit on our own. But
we can ask God to put us in the same boat as those
who do. And who are they? The righteous, the pious,
the elders, the scholars, and converts to Judaism.

Judaism, with all its ancient traditions and (literally)
tribal distinctions, is really a meritocracy. We do not
ask to be lumped together with the high priests or the
descendants of the royal line of David. We ask to be
considered like the people we all know who are
righteous and pious. We ask to be thought of like the
elders even when we do not evince much wisdom.
We ask to be thrown in with the great rabbinic
scholars, who delved into Torah learning and who
shared that learning with the people. And we ask to
be regarded as if we were true proselytes; that is,
converts to Judaism.

We don't always succeed in being righteous and pious, or in being wise like elders or scholars. But in the modern world, where it is easy for Jews to stop being Jews, in a sense we are all like converts to Judaism, which is to say that we are now all Jews by choice. Or at least we can be: we can (and must) decide, actively, to be Jews and to grow our Jewish knowledge and practice.

True proselytes have seen the world and have chosen Judaism. And that describes most of us who were born Jews, too.

We don't have to be kings or priests. All we have to be is Jews who choose Judaism.

Shma Koleinu

Heather G. Stoltz

שְׁמַע קוֹלֵנוּ, יְיָ אֱלֹהֵינוּ, חוּס וְרַחֵם עָלֵינוּ, וְקַבֵּל בְּרַחֲמִים וּבְרָצוֹן אֶת תְּפִלָּתֵנוּ, כִּי אֵל שׁוֹמֵעַ תְּפִלּוֹת וְתַחֲנוּנִים אָתָּה, וּמִלְּפָנֶיךָ, מַלְכֵּנוּ, רֵיקָם אַל תְּשִׁיבֵנוּ. כִּי אַתָּה שׁוֹמֵעַ תְּפִלַּת עַמְּךָ יִשְׂרָאֵל בְּרַחֲמִים . בָּרוּךְ אַתָּה יְיָ, שׁוֹמֵעַ תְּפִלָּה.

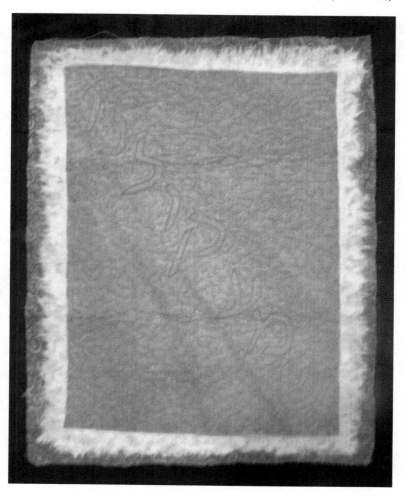

Three times a day, Jews ask God to *Shma Koleinu* (hear our voice). We plead with God to accept our prayer and not turn us away. Every day, as I recite these words, I know that God is listening and that, even through all of the chaos and walls that I have built up to protect myself, God is able to hear my deepest and most pure prayers.

This quilt depicts the darkness, chaos, and seeming pointlessness of everyday life. Although the hectic threads of daily routine hold things together, they can only do so much and the parts that should remain hidden spill out into the border, exposed and vulnerable. Yet through all this turmoil, the simple words of prayer come through pure and unharmed, reaching straight to God and calling God's light down into the chaos, comforting us with the knowledge that our prayers will be answered.

The Journal Quilt Project has given me the freedom to look inside and find a creative way to express my innermost thoughts, fears, and beliefs. My journal quilts have tracked my journey from despair to joy and have opened doors both inside myself and in the outside world. While I know that there is still a long road ahead, this project has opened my eyes to the path I need to follow. This quilt is a cry in the darkness, but it is also secure in the knowledge that the cry is heard and will be answered.

Shma Koleinu

Rabbi Steven A. Schwarzman

The working title for this book was *Ordinary Prayers,* because it got started when I saw how deeply ordinary people get into Jewish prayer.

And then I realized that this book had a natural title, taken from the *siddur* itself: *Shma Koleinu.* Hear our voice. And it's a prayer straight from the *Amidah.*

It isn't Hear our *voices,* and for good reason, I think. We all think different thoughts in our prayers. But we say the same prayers. We pray, as it were, in one voice: the same voice that our ancestors used, going back as far as Jewish prayers go, and the same voice that our descendants will use, as far into the future as Jewish prayers will go.

> *Hear our voice, God, have mercy on us, and accept our prayer in mercy and willingly, because you are a God who hears prayers and supplications. Do not send us away empty-handed from you, because you hear the prayer of your people Israel in mercy.*

We pray, together with all Jews everywhere and in every time, in one voice. It is the same prayer. We all have our individual needs and ways of expressing our prayers. But the most important prayer of all is the prayer to be heard. And we all share that prayer.

Our tradition teaches that the prayer of a congregation can be more powerful than the prayers of individuals. When we engage in deep Jewish prayer, we join a congregation not only of the *minyan* around us, but of all Jews everywhere in all times.

Vetehezeinah Eineinu

Rabbi Steven A. Schwarzman

וְתֶחֱזֶינָה עֵינֵינוּ בְּשׁוּבְךָ לְצִיּוֹן בְּרַחֲמִים. בָּרוּךְ אַתָּה יְיָ, הַמַּחֲזִיר שְׁכִינָתוֹ לְצִיּוֹן.

May our eyes witness your return to Zion in mercy, we say to God.

Over the long centuries of exile from our land, the land of Israel, reality found its way into theology. We began to relegate the return to Zion to some far-off time when God would effect that return miraculously.

And while some who say this prayer probably continue to think of a return to Zion in such terms, the prayer itself tells us otherwise.

You see, for us to witness God's return, we have to be there. We can't see it if we're not there to see it. From afar, we can only hear about it.

God has God's work to do, and we have ours. We are not equal partners, but neither can we shirk our responsibilities – or willingly miss out on the miracle.

Zion has been restored, and the small country that is Israel is a humming laboratory of innovation and problem-solving, in ethical issues no less than in technology.

May we, ourselves, be privileged to witness this miracle and take part in it.

Modim

Rabbi Jack Bloom

מוֹדִים אֲנַחְנוּ לָךְ, שָׁאַתָּה הוּא, יְיָ אֱלֹהֵינוּ וֵאלֹהֵי אֲבוֹתֵינוּ, לְעוֹלָם וָעֶד,
צוּר חַיֵּינוּ, מָגֵן יִשְׁעֵנוּ, אַתָּה הוּא לְדוֹר וָדוֹר נוֹדֶה לְךָ וּנְסַפֵּר תְּהִלָּתֶךָ.
עַל חַיֵּינוּ הַמְּסוּרִים בְּיָדֶךָ, וְעַל נִשְׁמוֹתֵינוּ הַפְּקוּדוֹת לָךְ, וְעַל נִסֶּיךָ שֶׁבְּכָל
יוֹם עִמָּנוּ, וְעַל נִפְלְאוֹתֶיךָ וְטוֹבוֹתֶיךָ שֶׁבְּכָל עֵת, עֶרֶב וָבֹקֶר וְצָהֳרָיִם,
הַטּוֹב כִּי לֹא כָלוּ רַחֲמֶיךָ, וְהַמְרַחֵם כִּי לֹא תַמּוּ חֲסָדֶיךָ מֵעוֹלָם קִוִּינוּ
לָךְ.

We are grateful to You, Adonai our God and God of our ancestors throughout all time. You are the Rock of our lives, our shield in every generation. We thank you and praise You for our lives that are in Your hand, for our souls that are in Your charge, for your miracles that daily attend us, and for your wonders and gifts that accompany us evening, morning, and noon. You are good, Your mercy everlasting; You are compassionate, Your kindness never-ending. We have always placed our hope in You.

Modim

Linda Friedman

I "thankfully acknowledge that You are the source of my strength", that "our lives are in Your hand, our souls are in Your care", for the miracles of my children and grandchildren – "morning, noon, and night." "You are my abiding hope."

Retzeh (On Shabbat)

Rabbi Jack Bloom

אֱלֹהֵינוּ וֵאלֹהֵי אֲבוֹתֵינוּ, רְצֵה נָא בִמְנוּחָתֵנוּ, קַדְּשֵׁנוּ בְּמִצְוֹתֶיךָ וְתֵן
חֶלְקֵנוּ בְּתוֹרָתֶךָ, שַׂבְּעֵנוּ מִטּוּבֶךָ וְשַׂמְּחֵנוּ בִּישׁוּעָתֶךָ, וְטַהֵר לִבֵּנוּ לְעָבְדְּךָ
בֶּאֱמֶת, וְהַנְחִילֵנוּ יְיָ אֱלֹהֵינוּ בְּאַהֲבָה וּבְרָצוֹן שַׁבַּת קָדְשֶׁךָ, וְיָנוּחוּ בוֹ כָּל
יִשְׂרָאֵל מְקַדְּשֵׁי שְׁמֶךָ. בָּרוּךְ אַתָּה יְיָ, מְקַדֵּשׁ הַשַּׁבָּת:

In the sixteenth century, Moses Mintz of Hamburg said that the ideal *Shaliah Tzibbur* (prayer leader) should be "blameless in character, humble, a general favorite and married; should be able to read easily and understand all the books of the Holy Scriptures; be the first to enter and the last to leave the house of God, and strive to attain the highest degree of devotion in his prayers. He should dress neatly and wear a long garment and knee breeches. And he should not look about him nor under his mantle. And he shouldn't move his hands restlessly but he should keep them folded neatly. And outside God's house, he should avoid sowing any seeds of anger or hatred against himself by keeping aloof from all communal disputes."

For anyone responsible for liturgy, that's one big challenge – but not the important one.

What is our challenge in the future? How we meet that challenge may well determine our future!

The *Shaliah Tzibur* came out of an era when there were few prayer books. One person who knew was appointed to lead, perhaps to chant (since melody held memory longer.) One could fulfill one's obligation by saying *amen* to what the *Shatz* was saying or chanting. So we have the tradition of *barukh hu uvarukh shmo* - Blessed Be He and Blessed Be His Name, and Amen. The *Shaliah Tzibur* acted together with the congregation as one responsive entity.

We live in a different time. We have lost the art of public worship. We have failed. How do we create a praying community while honoring the symbols of our past?

Which of those symbols still live? Which can be given life? Which are dead in this era? We must decide and know what we will include and what we will omit:

- That Torah needs to be taught, but the worship service is not a classroom.
- That music is crucial, but prayer is not a concert.
- That singing is needed, but worship is more than a songfest.
- That words are to be read, but worship is more than reading.
- That Hebrew is indispensable, but it alone is not enough.
- That aesthetics are crucial, but a service is not art for art's sake.
- That responsive reading is deadly, and must be transformed to responsive prayer.
- That repetition is intrinsic to ritual, and that obsessive repetition can kill the spirit.

- That Cantor and Rabbi are performers, yet worship is not a show.
- That Cantor and Rabbi and Congregation must be a single, balanced, responsive entity – one missing part destroys the whole enterprise.
- That room must be made for silent prayer, and that the silence not be empty.
- That we need to be loyal to the past, and not give the past a veto.
- That if you can't do it in two hours, you can't do it in 2½.
- And paradoxically, that longer is not better, except when it is.
- We need to know that timing is everything.
- That finding the balance of a right length of time for prayer – not too much, not too little – is like being a tightrope walker, maintaining one's balance by constant movement back and forth.
- That without community, we are finished, and yet we must make room for each individual's uniqueness.
- That we must use the intellect in creating worship where words that come from the heart enter the heart.

We need to create a worship experience recognizably Jewish in all its parts, without the detritus of the past. Old is not necessarily better.

We do achieve occasional success – sometimes inadvertently. This is our challenge. It is hard work, and vital to our future.

Birkat Kohanim – The Priestly Blessing

Rabbi Steven A. Schwarzman

אֱלֹהֵינוּ וֵאלֹהֵי אֲבוֹתֵינוּ, בָּרְכֵנוּ בַבְּרָכָה הַמְשֻׁלֶּשֶׁת בַּתּוֹרָה הַכְּתוּבָה עַל
יְדֵי מֹשֶׁה עַבְדֶּךָ, הָאֲמוּרָה מִפִּי אַהֲרֹן וּבָנָיו כֹּהֲנִים עַם קְדוֹשֶׁךָ,
כָּאָמוּר.

יְבָרֶכְךָ יְיָ וְיִשְׁמְרֶךָ.

יָאֵר יְיָ פָּנָיו אֵלֶיךָ וִיחֻנֶּךָּ.

יִשָּׂא יְיָ פָּנָיו אֵלֶיךָ וְיָשֵׂם לְךָ שָׁלוֹם.

I'm not a priest, a *kohen*. How do I know? Because my father isn't. Our identity as Jews comes from our mothers, but our tribal identity within the Jewish people comes from our fathers.

And so I am on the receiving end of the priestly blessing when it is given. In the Diaspora, the priests go up to bless the people only on holidays; in Israel, they do it every day.

If the *kohanim* don't give the blessing, the prayer leader does, using the introductory text above before the blessing:

> *Our God and God of our ancestors, bless us with the three-fold blessing in the Torah written by Moses your servant, spoken by Aaron and his sons the priests, your holy people.*

When the prayer leader says this blessing, it's really just a reference to how it is when the *kohanim* do it.

The real blessing, and the drama of it, is when the *kohanim* go up to bless the congregation. The prayer leader prompts them, word by word, and they – well, they don't actually bless the congregation themselves. What they do is channel God's blessing to us. It's a powerful moment. Children hide under their father's *tallit*, a sort of protective shield from the high voltage of this blessing. I always did this with my kids, and when they were small they would giggle a bit at this hide-and-seek game in *shul*.

And it *is* a high voltage ceremony. The *kohanim*, who a moment ago were regular members of the congregation, who might work as accountants or car repair guys, step out of their shoes and into their role as priests of Israel in a ritual that is several thousand years old. They cover themselves with their *tallitot*, extend their arms, and turn from side to side as they chant God's blessing to us. For our part, we refrain from looking directly at them, so as not to distract them.

And we receive God's blessing.

Receiving a blessing isn't always easy. It takes focus and humility and an openness to blessing – something that we might repress in a tough world as a protective measure.

But just as it is the *kohen*'s job to give us God's blessing, it is ours to receive it. It's the same blessing that parents give their children on Friday nights, and the parallel is clear. We need to regain some of that child-like innocence to be able to receive God's blessing. And being able to do so is a pretty incredible thing.

Sim Shalom

Rabbi Steven A. Schwarzman

שִׂים שָׁלוֹם טוֹבָה וּבְרָכָה, חֵן נָחֶסֶד וְרַחֲמִים, עָלֵינוּ וְעַל כָּל יִשְׂרָאֵל
עַמֶּךָ. בָּרְכֵנוּ, אָבִינוּ, כֻּלָּנוּ כְּאֶחָד בְּאוֹר פָּנֶיךָ, כִּי בְאוֹר פָּנֶיךָ נָתַתָּ לָּנוּ, יְיָ
אֱלֹהֵינוּ, תּוֹרַת חַיִּים וְאַהֲבַת חֶסֶד, וּצְדָקָה וּבְרָכָה וְרַחֲמִים וְחַיִּים
וְשָׁלוֹם, וְטוֹב בְּעֵינֶיךָ לְבָרֵךְ אֶת עַמְּךָ יִשְׂרָאֵל בְּכָל עֵת וּבְכָל שָׁעָה
בִּשְׁלוֹמֶךָ.

(בעשי״ת: בְּסֵפֶר חַיִּים, בְּרָכָה, וְשָׁלוֹם, וּפַרְנָסָה טוֹבָה, נִזָּכֵר וְנִכָּתֵב
לְפָנֶיךָ, אֲנַחְנוּ וְכָל עַמְּךָ בֵּית יִשְׂרָאֵל, לְחַיִּים טוֹבִים וּלְשָׁלוֹם.)

בָּרוּךְ אַתָּה יְיָ, הַמְבָרֵךְ אֶת עַמּוֹ יִשְׂרָאֵל בַּשָּׁלוֹם.

In both the morning version of this final blessing in
the *Amidah* and in its evening parallel, *Shalom Rav*,
peace is something that comes *upon* us. Not within us,
not among us, and certainly not from us. Peace comes
from above.

> *Place peace upon us, along with goodness and
> blessing and grace and kindness and mercy, upon
> us and upon all Israel, Your people.*

Why does peace need to come from above?

Perhaps because peace is not a standalone product. It
comes as part of a package. And we define that
package as the prayer goes on:

> *Bless us, our Father, all of us as one, in the light of
> Your countenance, because it is through the light of
> Your countenance, Lord our God, that you gave us
> a Torah of life and a love of kindness, and justice
> and blessing and mercy and life itself and – peace.*

Peace comes only at the end of that long chain. You can't have peace if you don't have Torah and life and kindness. You can't have peace if you don't have justice and blessing and mercy and, again, life itself.

But if you are blessed with all of those, then you have a chance to be further blessed, with peace. It comes from God.

Elohai Netzor Leshoni

Rabbi Jack Bloom

אֱלֹהַי, נְצוֹר לְשׁוֹנִי מֵרָע. וּשְׂפָתַי מִדַּבֵּר מִרְמָה: וְלִמְקַלְלַי נַפְשִׁי תִדֹּם,
וְנַפְשִׁי כֶּעָפָר לַכֹּל תִּהְיֶה. פְּתַח לִבִּי בְּתוֹרָתֶךָ, וּבְמִצְוֹתֶיךָ תִּרְדּוֹף נַפְשִׁי.
וְכָל הַחוֹשְׁבִים עָלַי רָעָה, מְהֵרָה הָפֵר עֲצָתָם וְקַלְקֵל מַחֲשַׁבְתָּם. עֲשֵׂה
לְמַעַן שְׁמֶךָ, עֲשֵׂה לְמַעַן יְמִינֶךָ, עֲשֵׂה לְמַעַן קְדֻשָּׁתֶךָ. עֲשֵׂה לְמַעַן
תּוֹרָתֶךָ. לְמַעַן יֵחָלְצוּן יְדִידֶיךָ, הוֹשִׁיעָה יְמִינְךָ וַעֲנֵנִי. יִהְיוּ לְרָצוֹן אִמְרֵי
פִי וְהֶגְיוֹן לִבִּי לְפָנֶיךָ, יְיָ צוּרִי וְגוֹאֲלִי. עֹשֶׂה שָׁלוֹם בִּמְרוֹמָיו, הוּא יַעֲשֶׂה
שָׁלוֹם עָלֵינוּ, וְעַל כָּל יִשְׂרָאֵל וְאִמְרוּ׃ אָמֵן.

My God, keep my tongue from evil, my lips from lies.
Help me ignore those who slander me. Open my
heart to your Torah, that I may pursue your *mitzvot*.
Frustrate the designs of those who plot evil against
me. Make nothing of their schemes.

A prayer from the heart, for the heart. From the soul,
for the soul. The quintessential personal prayer.

Here, the slanderers, the plotters of evil are not found
among those who share our planet. They are "aliens"
who, subsequent to psychological and/or emotional
pain, have taken up residence in us. Similar to
bacteria or viruses, though we host them, they are not
us.

Our psychological immune system, impaired by
psychic violence, though struggling valiantly, is
unable to reject them. In moments of vulnerability,
the "aliens," though not us, denigrate, demean, and
alienate us.

They tell us that we are not good enough, that we are frauds, that there is no room in the world for the likes of us, that we never do anything right, and on and on.

Though masquerading in our voice, and mimicking our style, they are not us; the evidence being that their attack leaves us diminished and alienated.

Created in the image of God, nothing that is authentically us would leave us demeaned, diminished, and alienated.

So we pray for Torah, compassion, holiness, and Torah yet again; teaching and reminding us that we are created in the breath-taking image of God, and that the aliens are most assuredly not us. And that peace be the sign of our healing.

Elohai Netzor Leshoni

Rabbi Steven A. Schwarzman

At the end of the *Amidah*, the core of all Jewish prayer, we add a meditative paragraph that is, perhaps, the "doorknob conversation" of our prayer. Doorknob conversations, as rabbis, pastors of all faiths, and therapists can tell you, are when the conversation is ostensibly over, and the agenda has been covered. On the way out, with a hand on the doorknob, the person turns his or her head back with one more thing that they almost forgot to mention.

And this "one more thing" turns out to be the real thing, the one thing that was on their mind the whole time. Disguised by the casualness with which it is presented, this request is what really calls out for attention and therapeutic help.

So what is the first thing we mention with our hands on the doorknob, on the way out of our *Amidah*? *Elohai, netzor leshoni meira usfatai midaber mirmah.* My God, keep my tongue from evil and my lips from speaking lies.

How's that again? We just got through a powerful prayer experience, pouring our hearts out to God, and now we're asking God to help us stop lying?

I think there is a profound truth in this meditation. It is our doorknob prayer. Yes, God, we need all the things we asked about during the *Amidah*: rain so crops can grow, life (in this world and the next), intelligence, Torah, forgiveness, redemption, and all the rest.

But you know what we really need, God? We need your help, because we know, and you know, that our prayers must sound like outrageous lies. We go through them without the focus they deserve. We say words that we don't fully understand or believe. We ask you for things that we don't do our part of the work in bringing about. And so often, so, so often, we look to our prayers as little more than incantations, verbal amulets, that if we just mouth them, you will be obligated somehow to obey us instead of the other way around. If that's not scandalous, what is?

This is why, God, we need your help, first and foremost, to learn to stop our verbal misdeeds. If you could help us purify our hearts, and our tongues to more purely express what's really in our hearts, then we would be so much closer to redemption. We would then be so much more able to ignore the bad thoughts that other people sometimes express about us or to us, because we would be better able to stay focused on what really counts and not be so enslaved to public opinion.

As the meditation continues, God can then open our hearts to Torah and help our souls pursue God's *mitzvot* (instead of all that other stuff that we often pursue).

Is this meditation a modern prayer? Hardly. It comes straight from the Talmud, at the end of the second chapter of Tractate Berakhot, combining the prayers of several of the ancient rabbis. If *they* felt a need to compose – and say – this meditation, we need feel no hesitation in saying it ourselves. With God's help, may our prayers be true, and may our words to ourselves and to others also be true.

Chapter 6
Tahanun –
Supplications

On ordinary weekdays (with some exceptions), right after the spiritual elevation of the *Amidah*, we deflate ourselves, in a good way, I think, and recite the supplications of *Tahanun*. We bow, vestigially, to God whose presence we have just tried to approach. We recognize that it was rather *hutzpadik* (presumptuous) of us to even try. We confess the frailty of our human endeavors and ask God to help us nonetheless.

– *Rabbi Steven A. Schwarzman*

Tahanun

Stephen Griffiths

וַיֹּאמֶר דָּוִד אֶל גָּד, צַר לִי מְאֹד, נִפְּלָה נָּא בְיַד יְיָ, כִּי רַבִּים רַחֲמָיו וּבְיַד
אָדָם אַל אֶפֹּלָה:

רַחוּם וְחַנּוּן חָטָאתִי לְפָנֶיךָ, יְיָ מָלֵא רַחֲמִים, רַחֵם עָלַי וְקַבֵּל תַּחֲנוּנָי:
יְיָ אַל בְּאַפְּךָ תוֹכִיחֵנִי, וְאַל בַּחֲמָתְךָ תְיַסְּרֵנִי: חָנֵּנִי יְיָ כִּי אֻמְלַל אָנִי,
רְפָאֵנִי יְיָ, כִּי נִבְהֲלוּ עֲצָמָי: וְנַפְשִׁי נִבְהֲלָה מְאֹד, וְאַתָּה יְיָ עַד מָתָי:
שׁוּבָה יְיָ חַלְּצָה נַפְשִׁי, הוֹשִׁיעֵנִי לְמַעַן חַסְדֶּךָ: כִּי אֵין בַּמָּוֶת זִכְרֶךָ,
בִּשְׁאוֹל מִי יוֹדֶה לָּךְ: יָגַעְתִּי בְּאַנְחָתִי, אַשְׂחֶה בְכָל לַיְלָה מִטָּתִי,
בְּדִמְעָתִי עַרְשִׂי אַמְסֶה: עָשְׁשָׁה מִכַּעַס עֵינִי, עָתְקָה בְּכָל צוֹרְרָי: סוּרוּ
מִמֶּנִּי כָּל פֹּעֲלֵי אָוֶן, כִּי שָׁמַע יְיָ קוֹל בִּכְיִי: שָׁמַע יְיָ תְּחִנָּתִי, יְיָ תְּפִלָּתִי
יִקָּח: יֵבֹשׁוּ וְיִבָּהֲלוּ מְאֹד כָּל אֹיְבָי, יָשֻׁבוּ יֵבֹשׁוּ רָגַע:

I said a *Shehehiyanu* the other day. No, not for Purim or any public occasion, but for a very private one instead. We are all on our individual Jewish journeys. Mine took a new direction about this time last year when I began to include the *Tahanun* prayers when laying *tefillin* each morning.

For anyone not familiar with these prayers, there is a whole raft of rules that govern when to say them and equally when not to say them. Plus on Mondays and Thursdays all 8-pages worth (in my Singer's Siddur) are said, but on Mondays, Wednesdays, Fridays and Sundays, a shortened version is said. Our Patriarchs who decided on all this had obviously not heard of the KISS principle.

I am no Hebrew grammarian, but I do like to know what it is I am saying. Thus, my first excursion into these prayers saw me taking them paragraph by paragraph, trying reasonably successfully to match the Hebrew with what seemed to be a fair translation into English. Crumbs, it was hard work at times! The pages seemed filled with victimhood, affliction, fear of abandonment, yearning, sorrow, guilt and constant pleading for forgiveness *l'ma'an shmekha*, for thy name's sake. Most of this was expressed in complex-looking Hebrew constructs matched by equally convoluted English translations.

Then, suddenly, came words of sheer simplicity in one short paragraph that set everything else into context and held, for me, a real meaning of why I would be saying these prayers at all. In my badly transliterated Hebrew, the paragraph read: *Rahum v'hanun hatati l'fanekha. Adonai malei rahamim, rahem alai v'kabel tahanunai*, which according to Singer's means:

> *Oh thou who art merciful and gracious, I have sinned before thee. Oh Lord, full of mercy, have mercy upon me and receive my supplication.*

Why it appears towards the end and not right at the beginning is a mystery to me. Here in a nutshell is the whole *raison d'être* for saying *Tahanun*. When I first read these words, both the almost poetic Hebrew and the more prosaic English, I was held spellbound by the sheer majesty of what they implied. Here was a simple confession and an equally simple request to be heard. No flowery language, no complex lists of sins, no angst, no hyperbole. Instead, a calm acceptance of one's frailty and a gentle expectation that words will be heard.

Another thought struck a few weeks later when I reached this point in the *Tahanun* prayers: Yom Kippur is not the only chance I have to express contrition and to seek to improve how I behave. Every day that *Tahanun* is said is like a mini-Yom Kippur.

Not that I am implying that I shall arrive at Yom Kippur proper free of any guilt for what I might have said or done. Far from it. I shall, though, have spent a year enjoying the comfort of simple yet powerful words that will have at least encouraged me in the thought that my words will have been heard.

Tahanun

Rabbi Peretz Rodman

וַיֹּאמֶר דָּוִד אֶל גָּד, צַר לִי מְאֹד, נִפְּלָה נָּא בְיַד יְיָ, כִּי רַבִּים רַחֲמָיו, וּבְיַד אָדָם אַל אֶפֹּלָה.

רַחוּם וְחַנּוּן, חָטָאתִי לְפָנֶיךָ, יְיָ מָלֵא רַחֲמִים, רַחֵם עָלַי וְקַבֵּל תַּחֲנוּנָי. יְיָ אַל בְּאַפְּךָ תוֹכִיחֵנִי, וְאַל בַּחֲמָתְךָ תְיַסְּרֵנִי. חָנֵּנִי יְיָ כִּי אֻמְלַל אָנִי, רְפָאֵנִי יְיָ, כִּי נִבְהֲלוּ עֲצָמָי. וְנַפְשִׁי נִבְהֲלָה מְאֹד, וְאַתָּה יְיָ עַד מָתָי. שׁוּבָה יְיָ חַלְּצָה נַפְשִׁי, הוֹשִׁיעֵנִי לְמַעַן חַסְדֶּךָ. כִּי אֵין בַּמָּוֶת זִכְרֶךָ, בִּשְׁאוֹל מִי יוֹדֶה לָּךְ. יָגַעְתִּי בְּאַנְחָתִי, אַשְׂחֶה בְכָל לַיְלָה מִטָּתִי, בְּדִמְעָתִי עַרְשִׂי אַמְסֶה. עָשְׁשָׁה מִכַּעַס עֵינִי, עָתְקָה בְּכָל צוֹרְרָי. סוּרוּ מִמֶּנִּי כָּל פֹּעֲלֵי אָוֶן, כִּי שָׁמַע יְיָ קוֹל בִּכְיִי. שָׁמַע יְיָ תְּחִנָּתִי, יְיָ תְּפִלָּתִי יִקָּח. יֵבֹשׁוּ וְיִבָּהֲלוּ מְאֹד כָּל אֹיְבָי, יָשֻׁבוּ יֵבֹשׁוּ רָגַע.

שׁוֹמֵר יִשְׂרָאֵל, שְׁמוֹר שְׁאֵרִית יִשְׂרָאֵל, וְאַל יֹאבַד יִשְׂרָאֵל, הָאוֹמְרִים שְׁמַע יִשְׂרָאֵל. שׁוֹמֵר גּוֹי אֶחָד, שְׁמוֹר שְׁאֵרִית עַם אֶחָד, וְאַל יֹאבַד גּוֹי אֶחָד, הַמְיַחֲדִים שִׁמְךָ יְיָ אֱלֹהֵינוּ יְיָ אֶחָד. שׁוֹמֵר גּוֹי קָדוֹשׁ, שְׁמוֹר שְׁאֵרִית עַם קָדוֹשׁ, וְאַל יֹאבַד גּוֹי קָדוֹשׁ, הַמְשַׁלְּשִׁים בְּשָׁלֹשׁ קְדֻשּׁוֹת לְקָדוֹשׁ. מִתְרַצֶּה בְּרַחֲמִים וּמִתְפַּיֵּס בְּתַחֲנוּנִים, הִתְרַצֶּה וְהִתְפַּיֵּס לְדוֹר עָנִי, כִּי אֵין עוֹזֵר. אָבִינוּ מַלְכֵּנוּ, חָנֵּנוּ וַעֲנֵנוּ, כִּי אֵין בָּנוּ מַעֲשִׂים, עֲשֵׂה עִמָּנוּ צְדָקָה וָחֶסֶד וְהוֹשִׁיעֵנוּ.

וַאֲנַחְנוּ לֹא נֵדַע מַה נַּעֲשֶׂה, כִּי עָלֶיךָ עֵינֵינוּ. זְכֹר רַחֲמֶיךָ יְיָ וַחֲסָדֶיךָ, כִּי מֵעוֹלָם הֵמָּה. יְהִי חַסְדְּךָ יְיָ עָלֵינוּ, כַּאֲשֶׁר יִחַלְנוּ לָךְ. אַל תִּזְכָּר לָנוּ עֲוֹנוֹת רִאשׁוֹנִים, מַהֵר יְקַדְּמוּנוּ רַחֲמֶיךָ, כִּי דַלּוֹנוּ מְאֹד. חָנֵּנוּ יְיָ חָנֵּנוּ, כִּי רַב שָׂבַעְנוּ בוּז. בְּרֹגֶז רַחֵם תִּזְכּוֹר. כִּי הוּא יָדַע יִצְרֵנוּ, זָכוּר כִּי עָפָר אֲנָחְנוּ. עָזְרֵנוּ אֱלֹהֵי יִשְׁעֵנוּ עַל דְּבַר כְּבוֹד שְׁמֶךָ, וְהַצִּילֵנוּ וְכַפֵּר עַל חַטֹּאתֵינוּ לְמַעַן שְׁמֶךָ.

Tahanun is the biggest "downer" of all the components of our daily liturgy, with its insistence on the individual's (that is, my) abhorrent sins and his (my!) abject dependence on divine grace in order to have any hope for even the smallest measure of forgiveness. For those who sing any part of the prayer – usually the *Shomer Yisrael* verses – the plaintive melodies underscore the mood of shame and self-abnegation bordering on depression.

For that reason, it is with a certain amount of embarrassment that I sometimes find myself chuckling my way through much of that part of the service. But if you read it closely, *Tahanun* may strike you, as it strikes me, as the funniest, most subtly sarcastic composition in our liturgy.

We start off asking to find ourselves delivered into God's hands when in distress. Citing 2 Samuel 24:14, we recite:

> *King David said to the prophet Gad: 'I am in deep distress. Let us fall into the hands of Adonai, whose compassion is great....'*

God has abundant capacity to forgive; people, however, are another story. The verse continues: "... but let me not fall into human hands." Please – we plead – whatever happens, don't let me come to need the support of human beings. The clear implication is: *them* you can count on at best to let you down, at worst to kick you when you're down. What SOBs those humans can be!

And then, not long after that invidious comparison, in which God comes out ahead of His fickle creatures, we proceed to take Him, too, down a notch. In the most poetic passage in *Tahanun*, we recite:

> *Guardian of Israel, guard the remnant of Israel; and preserve the people Israel, who proclaim: Shma Yisrael.*

> *Guardian of a unique people, guard the remnant of*
> *that unique people; and preserve the people who*
> *affirm: Adonai is our God, Adonai alone.*

> *Guardian of a holy people, guard the remnant of*
> *that holy people; and preserve that holy people, who*
> *chant in praise of the Holy One: Kadosh, Kadosh,*
> *Kadosh.*

Don't let the pious language fool you; there's a lot of attitude in that rhetoric. "Yo, Guardian of Israel!" we call out, "how 'bout making sure that what little is left of Your people Israel doesn't get done in as well?"

What are we to think about that guardian? He hasn't exactly been getting the job done, that's for sure. All that is left of the glorious House of Israel is just a *she'erit*, a remnant of past glory, a mere shard. We express that sentiment three times before adding that we are a *dor 'ani*, an "afflicted generation," because there is no one around to help us. From this we understand: You, Blessed Holy One, may have a spotty record, but You're all we've got, so please get Your act together this time.

Yes, it is embarrassing to be spotted chortling during *Tahanun*. But while I find that part of the *minyan* experience so humorous, it is, for all that, no less meaningful to me as a religious experience. Maybe more so, actually. A God whom I can needle and rib about doing His part for His people and His world may be the God most able to get me to pay attention when He gets serious with me and commands me to do my part as well.

Tahanun – Psalm 130

Rabbi Steven A. Schwarzman

שִׁיר הַמַּעֲלוֹת ːמִמַּעֲמַקִּים קְרָאתִיךָ יְהֹוָה.

אֲדֹנָי שִׁמְעָה בְקוֹלִי ː

תִּהְיֶינָה אָזְנֶיךָ קַשֻּׁבוֹת לְקוֹל תַּחֲנוּנָי.

אִם עֲוֹנוֹת תִּשְׁמָר יָהּ אֲדֹנָי, מִי יַעֲמֹד.

כִּי עִמְּךָ הַסְּלִיחָה לְמַעַן תִּוָּרֵא.

קִוִּיתִי יְהֹוָה קִוְּתָה נַפְשִׁי וְלִדְבָרוֹ הוֹחָלְתִּי.

נַפְשִׁי לַאדֹנָי מִשֹּׁמְרִים לַבֹּקֶר שֹׁמְרִים לַבֹּקֶר.

יַחֵל יִשְׂרָאֵל אֶל יְהֹוָה ː כִּי עִם יְהֹוָה הַחֶסֶד וְהַרְבֵּה עִמּוֹ פְדוּת.

וְהוּא יִפְדֶּה אֶת יִשְׂרָאֵל מִכֹּל עֲוֹנֹתָיו.

Sometimes, it is the mornings after not enough sleep that I'm the most aware of the words in the *siddur*, because my tired eyes and brain need to focus that much harder on what they might otherwise gloss over. And so, one morning, the end of this psalm (added to the traditional Psalm 6 in many Conservative siddurim) jumped out at me: *vehu yifdeh et yisrael mikol avonotav* – God will redeem Israel from all of its sins.

For thousands of times that I've read this, it sat there, waiting to jump up like a wildflower in the Negev standing by patiently for a few drops of rain every year or two before sprouting again. And then, one tired morning, there it was.

God will redeem Israel from all of its sins. That's an astounding theological statement. It sounds like God will, with grace, simply wipe away our sins. But it gets better. Rabbi David Kimhi, the medieval commentator known as Radak, notices the unusual verb. It doesn't say that God will *forgive* all our sins. It says that God will redeem us from them. If you were to say, how can God do this when I am so full of sin, it's actually a process. First, God forgives us for the sins we have committed in the past. Then God enables our hearts to find our way back to God with all our hearts. And then, in an act of redemption the way the word is usually understood, God will redeem us from our exile with mercy.

Forgiveness of sin is itself great, and even more so when it applies to all Israel. But when that forgiveness is just the first step toward our redemption, first as individuals and then as a people, it's truly gracious. May this redemption come speedily, in our days!

Avinu Malkeinu

Rabbi Steven A. Schwarzman

אָבִינוּ מַלְכֵּנוּ, חָנֵּנוּ וַעֲנֵנוּ כִּי אֵין בָּנוּ מַעֲשִׂים, עֲשֵׂה עִמָּנוּ צְדָקָה וָחֶסֶד
וְהוֹשִׁיעֵנוּ:

Jews who set foot in synagogues even once a year know this prayer. They also know the beautiful melody with which it is sung (though some know an alternate melody recorded and made famous by Barbra Streisand and others). Powerfully, at the end of the Yom Kippur service, congregations sing *Avinu Malkeinu* together with their cantors, pleading for one last chance at forgiveness, for one last chance at being inscribed and sealed in the book of life.

The funny thing is, it's not the only chance we get. *Avinu Malkeinu* is part of the daily liturgy, towards the end of the brief section of penitential prayers known as *Tahanun*. With some exceptions, we say this not just once a year, but every weekday.

Does that take the heartfelt nature of the prayer away? No, just as saying the daily prayers in a somewhat more matter-of-fact way than on Shabbat does not take away their import or how we relate to them. It's just that if Shabbat morning services take two or three hours, that's not a luxury we have at morning *minyan*, so by necessity we go more quickly through the prayers during the week.

On the face of it, *Avinu Malkeinu* asks God to have mercy on us and answer us even though our deeds are as nothing; even so, we plead, do with us justice and righteousness and save us.

But one can read the same words differently: *Avinu Malkeinu*, have mercy on us and answer us precisely because our deeds are as nothing. A subtle difference, perhaps, but real. In one reading, we admit that our deeds are relatively inconsequential, and that we can't rely on them in making our plea to God for mercy. In the other reading, we admit that our deeds really are as nothing. We waste so much time, we humans. There are so many good things we could be doing – but we're not. Yes, we busy ourselves with all kinds of activities that seem important. But deep down, we know that they are fleeting. And our lives are fleeting.

When we have the courage to see that life is real, and that our lives are finite, and how miserable a job we usually do in making good use of the time we are given, *that* is when we can say to God, in sincerity, have mercy on us and answer us even though, being human, we just don't have the good deeds to show. And then we continue: *aseh imanu tzedakah vahesed* - do with us, or perhaps even better, *make* with us, justice and righteousness. Save us from meaninglessness by helping us to do justice and righteousness. Save us, and we shall be saved.

Chapter 7
Torah Service

The Torah is read not only on Shabbat morning, but also on Shabbat afternoon, Monday and Thursday mornings, and on other occasions such as *Rosh Hodesh*.

You can see the relative importance of these days by the number of aliyot given to each when the Torah is read: Shabbat gets at least seven aliyot. Weekdays and Shabbat afternoon get three. *Rosh Hodesh* gets four, as do the intermediate days of *Pesah* and *Sukkot*. Festivals (think *Pesah, Shavuot,* and *Sukkot*) get five. So does *Rosh Hashanah. Yom Kippur* gets six.

Shabbat clearly is at the top of this hierarchy. But we can't go more than three days without Torah, so our tradition teaches that we need to read several times each week.

– *Rabbi Steven A. Schwarzman*

Adonai, Adonai (on Festivals)

Amy D. Goldstein

יְיָ, יְיָ, אֵל רַחוּם וְחַנּוּן, אֶרֶךְ אַפַּיִם וְרַב חֶסֶד וֶאֱמֶת: נֹצֵר חֶסֶד
לָאֲלָפִים, נֹשֵׂא עָוֹן וָפֶשַׁע וְחַטָּאָה, וְנַקֵּה:

Oh Lord, my God, merciful and gracious Ruler, slow to anger, and with abounding kindness and truth; granting lovingkindness to the thousandth generation, forgiving iniquity, transgression, and sin, and cleanses.

We affirm these two *pesukim* (Exodus 34:6-7) as we open the Ark during the Torah Service on a weekday holiday. Recited aloud as we look at the Torah, prior to removing it, they begin a short personal petitionary prayer cycle. Followed by a silent personal petition for aid in doing good in the world, rejecting evil impulses, being worthy of God's Torah, and meriting a place in the World to Come, this insertion concludes with a personal request that God accept the prayer – quoting Psalms (69:14), referring to one of the attributes of mercy, abundant lovingkindness.

We recite this prayer, one that God taught to Moses on Mt. Sinai, as we have opened the Divine Portal – the Ark – to speak directly to God, and to read in the Torah about our early relationship. Our recitation takes place as we look directly at God's gift to the Jewish People, the Torah, during a Divinely-ordained ritual celebration.

However, this is not a simple prayer constructed by the Sages in order to help us express our thoughts. Indeed, it is not the recitation of a Divinely-inspired Psalm, the words of Prophecy, or a descriptive portion of the Torah. God taught this prayer to Moses for Moses to teach to the Children of Israel, so that we can appeal for God's forgiveness.

God does so during one of the most intimate parts of the Torah. Moses is on Mt. Sinai speaking directly to God, face to face. Moses asks to see God's face – to understand God's Nature – and God states that a human cannot see God's face and live. Moses' longing is palpable, so God shields Moses' face and passes before Moses, revealing the back of God's Head – the part of God's nature that mankind can grasp.

Yet reciting this prayer is more than simply reminding God of an intimate moment. God – being outside of linear time and space – continuously and simultaneously inhabits all interactions in history that seem to humans as taking place on a temporal continuum. Thus, when we affirm this 13-faceted prayer, also called the 13 attributes of mercy, we actually inhabit the human part of this scene. *We* are on Mt. Sinai with God; *we* are being shielded by God; God is passing before *us* and revealing part of God's Nature to each Jewish person as we recite this prayer.

We affirm God's 13 attributes of mercy collectively in a *minyan*, yet also as individuals – just as the People of Israel stood *at* Sinai, while Moses stood *on* Sinai. Likewise, we stand in a congregation, but are each face to face with the Divine.

On these special occasions – the holy days that are not also Shabbat – God is in the process of judging our activities in the world vis-à-vis God's Commandments. God will either reward or punish – will our crops succeed or fail, will we have rain or drought, will we be prosperous or impoverished, will we live or die? Through these words, recalling God's merciful nature, both we and God relive the most tender moment of our millennia-long intimate partnership. Our relationship is renewed, and through God's infinite Mercy, we are blessed.

Misheberakh Leholim – A Prayer for Healing

Rabbi Lisa Gelber

מִי שֶׁבֵּרַךְ אֲבוֹתֵינוּ אַבְרָהָם יִצְחָק וְיַעֲקֹב, מֹשֶׁה אַהֲרֹן וּשְׁלֹמֹה, הוּא יְבָרֵךְ אֶת הַחוֹלֶה: לִזְכֹּר (פלוני) בֶּן (פלונית) בַּעֲבוּר שֶׁ(פלוני בן פלוני) יִתֵּן לִצְדָקָה בַּעֲבוּרוֹ. בִּשְׂכַר זֶה, הַקָּדוֹשׁ בָּרוּךְ הוּא יִמָּלֵא רַחֲמִים עָלָיו, לְהַחֲלִימוֹ וּלְרַפֹּאתוֹ וּלְהַחֲזִיקוֹ וּלְהַחֲיוֹתוֹ, וְיִשְׁלַח לוֹ מְהֵרָה רְפוּאָה שְׁלֵמָה מִן הַשָּׁמַיִם, לִרְמַ״ח אֵבָרָיו, וּשְׁסָ״ה גִּידָיו, בְּתוֹךְ שְׁאָר חוֹלֵי יִשְׂרָאֵל, רְפוּאַת הַנֶּפֶשׁ, וּרְפוּאַת הַגּוּף, [שַׁבָּת הִיא] [יוֹם טוֹב הִיא] מִלִּזְעֹק וּרְפוּאָה קְרוֹבָה לָבֹא, הַשְׁתָּא בַּעֲגָלָא וּבִזְמַן קָרִיב. וְנֹאמַר אָמֵן.

A visitor takes away a sixtieth of the illness.
(Talmud, Bava Metzia 30b)

Three days after my 34th birthday, I arose early in the morning and made my way to Harborview Medical Center. The date remains fixed in my mind less because of my surgery than because of a young woman I met during my initial days of recovery in the hospital. I'll call her "Emily."

Despite all the time I'd spent in hospital settings, I had never stayed overnight as a patient. Selfishly, I wanted my own room – a rare commodity these days. I anticipated wanting to be alone following the surgery. I had no interest in hearing about someone else's diagnosis or game plan for healing. The last thing I wanted was for someone else's misfortune and recovery to get in the way of the little control I might have over my own physical space.

Yet, even as I focused on my own needs and as I set goals for getting up and out of the hospital, I could not ignore the young woman in the bed by the window. Seven weeks before, Emily had survived an accident that left her, at least for the time being, unable to walk. The first day, I introduced myself and we exchanged names. The second day, she asked my age, and we shared that small piece of our personal narratives. Other than those brief exchanges, we didn't really talk.

As time wore on, her presence, for me, grew in the room. Every time I got out of bed to do something as mundane as walk down the hall or brush my teeth, I thought of Emily's ability to maintain her dignity while lying in that hospital bed at the mercy of those assigned to see to her well-being.

As someone who impresses upon people the importance of advocating for oneself in the hospital, or finding someone to advocate on one's behalf, I came fairly well equipped to speak my mind. I was also blessed with a caring medical staff who treated me as a patient and a person with feelings and opinions in the process of healing. I didn't know anything about Emily's background and experiences – who and how she was before her accident; I continually marveled at her ability to maintain her sense of self and speak her mind under what must have been the most excruciating of circumstances.

Three days after my surgery, I got out of bed, got dressed, and prepared to leave the hospital. My parents chatted quietly in the hallway with Emily's mother. As I waited for the wheelchair driver assigned to escort me to the lobby to arrive, I quietly walked over to Emily's side of the room. I don't know if she knew I was a rabbi. My doctors called me "Lisa," at my request, and while one nurse called me "rabbi, lady," my title and chosen work remained pretty much unspoken. My status in the Jewish community aside, as I stood beside Emily's bed, I was engaged in a powerful act of *hesed* available to us all, that of *bikkur holim*, literally, "visiting the sick."

Bikkur holim takes many forms, both spoken and silent; one of its most powerful goals is to be present and, in that presence, mitigate another's pain. The ability to bring healing, the opportunity to enhance someone's spiritual well-being in time of physical or emotional stress, is one of the most profound gifts we have to offer one another. None of us can truly know someone else's pain and suffering. By putting aside our own needs and quieting our internal dialogue, we create safe space to bring comfort and invite God's presence in.

After sharing with Emily how much her courage had strengthened me, I hesitated for a moment. Part of me wanted to utter the brief words of Moses on behalf of his sister Miriam when she is stricken with leprosy, "*El na refah na lah.*" "Please, God, bless her with healing." Yet I feared that within this context it might be seen as gratuitous, designed to meet my need for offering healing. And so, instead, I explained to Emily the Jewish practice of offering blessings for those in need of healing during our synagogue service and asked if we might do that for her. Her eyes filled with tears, as did mine, as she agreed and thanked me for my kindness throughout our time as roommates. It seems that even in our silence, I too had offered her some strength.

While I had wondered briefly about starting a new year of life with the physical and emotional trauma of surgery, had I chosen another day or even another time for my surgery, I would likely never have met Emily. Even within my own pain and work towards healing, she reminded me of the responsibility we have as Jews to pay attention to those around us, reaching deep within to garner the strength and courage to help one another, becoming ourselves a blessing and helping others, truly, to live.

Misheberakh Leholim – A Prayer for Healing

Rabbi Samuel Barth

If an anthropology student from the University of Mars were to attend a Shabbat morning service in an American Jewish synagogue, what kind of understanding about our real synagogue lives might emerge in the student's term paper on the topic? The essay might suggest that announcements and *kiddush* are the most important parts of the experience because that is when the most people are present. The Martian professor (whose appearance we will not explore here) might urge the student to be more subtle and to observe closely the body language of the human participants to discern which parts of the service are most engaging and important to those present.

When I invite my students at JTS to identify which parts of the Shabbat morning service are most important to congregants, the first response from the class is often a theological (or *halakhic*) Top Ten— including the *Shma*; the *Amidah*; the sermon (from rabbinical students); the *Kedushah* (from cantorial students); and, sometimes, the Mourners' *Kaddish*.

Then I ask them to think about the atmosphere at certain points—body language, attentiveness, focus, and sometimes open tears—and there is often significant (but never total) agreement that the *Mi*

Sheberakh (prayer for healing) attracts the greatest engagement and attention from the congregation. This is a relatively new phenomenon that would not have been observed even a generation ago, even though it was not uncommon for a congregant with a sick relative to ask that a *Mi Sheberakh* be recited by the *hazzan*, rabbi, or *gabbai*. The well-known text and musical composition by Rabbi Drorah Setel and Debbie Friedman (z"l) have certainly added greatly to the experience of many congregations, but the importance of the *Mi Sheberakh* is palpable in synagogues where that text and melody are unknown.

The liturgical text of healing from the daily *Amidah* addresses itself to healing of "body and soul." I suggest that the importance of this text, with its many rituals and melodies, grows out of a yearning among many contemporary Jews to bring their deepest experience, their inner pain, into the synagogue. Many of our texts and practices are of great antiquity, with profound depths of meaning—and are also arcane and hard to understand. We all understand illness and healing, and—theologically problematic though it might be—we can all imagine praying to an omnipotent God that our beloved friends and family members find healing of body, mind, and soul.

We recall that Moses prayed for his sister, Miriam; that Elijah prayed for a dying child; and that many Sages prayed for their colleagues and students and members of the community. Healing is in part a well understood medical science, but also a mystery.

During the week, we turn to physicians and healers with their sciences and arts. On *Shabbat* and in prayer, we confront the mystery among our community, in the presence of the Torah, and always in the presence of God.

Prayer for Israel's Soldiers

Rabbi Peretz Rodman

The One who blessed our ancestors… — may He bless the soldiers of the Israel Defense Forces, who stand guard over our country … on land, in the air, and at sea…

So begins a brief prayer recited in Israeli synagogues — outside the ultra-Orthodox sector — and in some synagogues abroad. In Israel, no one needs to instruct the congregation to stand: we are former soldiers, the parents of soldiers, or soldiers ourselves.

Hearing those words, I am in awe of what my children have been asked to give to their country. I am humbled by their willingness to serve for years, to volunteer extra years, to push themselves beyond their imagined limits—and to feel pride in doing so.

Sometimes soldiers on leave are present. Not long ago, they were children who played among us. Now they shift their weight and look to the floor, avoiding the proud gaze of parents and friends. None is in uniform. When they came through the doors of their homes, they went straight to their bedrooms and donned civilian clothes. Unwritten rules brook no puffery or pride about military service. Captains and privates, often on a first-name basis in uniform, are invariably equal on weekends.

... May the LORD cause our enemies who rise up against us to be repelled before them. May the blessed Holy One protect and rescue our soldiers from all danger and trouble, from all injury and illness, and grant blessing and success to all their deeds...

That sentiment is felt deeply by all present, as is the continuation, which asks that they be crowned with salvation and victory. But I bristle at the words that precede that thought:

... and may He exterminate our enemies beneath them.

The sentiment recalls Psalm 47:4, "The LORD... subjects peoples beneath us, sets nations beneath our feet." The biblical verb for "subject" today means "exterminate." The thought of war as divine pest control is jarring, and defies Ezekiel's message (18:23), "Is it my desire that a wicked person shall die?—says the LORD God. It is rather that he shall turn back from his ways and live." The late Rabbi Shmuel Avigdor Hacohen claimed to have authored this prayer—without the offensive clause, which he attributed to chief IDF Rabbi Shlomo Goren, adding, "I would never have written such a thing!"

I never say those words.

Partial recompense for the bellicose thought I must endure hearing comes sometimes at the end of this prayer: the wish that our soldiers witness the fulfillment of the promise of the high priest before the Israelite armies after exhorting them to have courage:

For it is the LORD your God who marches with you to do battle for you with your enemy, to bring you salvation (Deut. 20:4).

Many times this verse is intoned with careless phrasing, making the closing sentiment: "with your enemy to bring you salvation." In Israel's predicament, our salvation can indeed come only with that of our enemies, not by their extermination.

Vezos (Vezot) HaTorah

Joan Gaffin

וְזֹאת הַתּוֹרָה אֲשֶׁר שָׂם מֹשֶׁה לִפְנֵי בְּנֵי יִשְׂרָאֵל עַל פִּי יְיָ בְּיַד מֹשֶׁה :

As a child growing up at a Yeshiva, women did not participate in prayer on the *bimah*. Now, as an adult, I am in awe of women who can conduct and participate in prayer services. I myself have been blessed to participate in the *hagbah* service (the lifting of the Torah after it is read) twice during Sisterhood Shabbat. I feel excitement coming to my mind, body and heart when I remember these memories. I have excitement in my heart waiting for the raising of the Torah for the congregation to witness.

The prayer *Vezos Hatorah* and *hagbah* are very powerful spiritually. When we as a congregation speak these words, I feel Hashem deep in my heart. I see and feel Hashem's light pouring down from the heavens – the light beaming down on the *bimah*, then spreading throughout the congregation like a wave. I feel overwhelmed in my body, my mind and in my heart. I pray that others feel Hashem's power flowing through their bodies as I do.

When we pray in numbers with strength in our hearts, the light of God spreads throughout the universe for all to feel. When we feel the love, the joy, the peace, the beauty, and the truth, a feeling I can barely describe comes upon me; possible words are heavenly, joyful, and miraculous. I have hope and faith that all will feel these feelings in prayer!

Aheinu Kol Beit Yisrael

Rabbi Steven A. Schwarzman

יְהִי רָצוֹן מִלְּפְנֵי אָבִינוּ שֶׁבַּשָּׁמַיִם, לְכוֹנֵן אֶת בֵּית חַיֵּינוּ, וּלְהָשִׁיב אֶת שְׁכִינָתוֹ בְּתוֹכֵנוּ, בִּמְהֵרָה בְּיָמֵינוּ, וְנֹאמַר אָמֵן.
יְהִי רָצוֹן מִלְּפְנֵי אָבִינוּ שֶׁבַּשָּׁמַיִם, לְרַחֵם עָלֵינוּ וְעַל פְּלֵיטָתֵנוּ, וְלִמְנֹעַ מַשְׁחִית וּמַגֵּפָה מֵעָלֵינוּ וּמֵעַל כָּל עַמּוֹ בֵּית יִשְׂרָאֵל, וְנֹאמַר אָמֵן.
יְהִי רָצוֹן מִלְּפְנֵי אָבִינוּ שֶׁבַּשָּׁמַיִם, לְקַיֵּם בָּנוּ חַכְמֵי יִשְׂרָאֵל, הֵם וּנְשֵׁיהֶם וּבְנֵיהֶם וּבְנוֹתֵיהֶם, וְתַלְמִידֵיהֶם וְתַלְמִידֵי תַלְמִידֵיהֶם, בְּכָל מְקוֹמוֹת מוֹשְׁבוֹתֵיהֶם, וְנֹאמַר אָמֵן.
יְהִי רָצוֹן מִלְּפְנֵי אָבִינוּ שֶׁבַּשָּׁמַיִם, שֶׁנִּשְׁמַע וְנִתְבַּשֵּׂר בְּשׂוֹרוֹת טוֹבוֹת יְשׁוּעוֹת וְנֶחָמוֹת, וִיקַבֵּץ נִדָּחֵינוּ מֵאַרְבַּע כַּנְפוֹת הָאָרֶץ, וְנֹאמַר אָמֵן.

אַחֵינוּ כָּל בֵּית יִשְׂרָאֵל, הַנְּתוּנִים בְּצָרָה וּבַשִּׁבְיָה, הָעוֹמְדִים בֵּין בַּיָּם וּבֵין בַּיַּבָּשָׁה, הַמָּקוֹם יְרַחֵם עֲלֵיהֶם, וְיוֹצִיאֵם מִצָּרָה לִרְוָחָה, וּמֵאֲפֵלָה לְאוֹרָה, וּמִשִּׁעְבּוּד לִגְאֻלָּה, הַשְׁתָּא בַּעֲגָלָא וּבִזְמַן קָרִיב, וְנֹאמַר אָמֵן.

It's not a new prayer. The Torah has been lifted after the reading, and is being wrapped. The *shaliah tzibur* usually squeezes in this prayer, and several before it, during this time, so as to allow the weekday *minyan* to finish on time for people to get to work.

And in this last paragraph, the congregation joins in.

The previous prayers ask for God's mercy to rebuild the Temple, to have mercy on us and keep us from pestilence, to establish Torah scholars (along with their students and families), and to let us hear the good news of our ingathering from the four corners of the earth.

But this last paragraph is different. It uses different language. And its subject is different. We ask God to have mercy on Jews who are in distress or captivity, to bring them to freedom and light and redemption, speedily in our days.

In many periods in history, Jews were taken hostage, so much so that there is a developed body of *halakhah* on how much ransom the community should pay the captors so as not to inflate the price the next time.

And, sadly, we see this in our own day as well, when Israel's enemies capture IDF soldiers – including ones they have killed, because they know that Israel does not abandon its people – and hold them hostage for years at a time.

> *Our brothers, the entire House of Israel, given to distress and captivity, who are on the sea or the land, may the Source have mercy on them, and bring them out of their straits to welfare, from darkness to light, from slavery to redemption, speedily and soon, and let us say Amen.*

This prayer is different. And it's not new. The enemies of Israel and the Jewish people seem to find new levels of cruelty, kidnapping, killing randomly – randomly, that is, except that the target is anyone who happens to be Israeli or Jewish.

May God, who is the Source of peace, bring peace to the captives and their families. And may the captives be redeemed, from darkness to light, speedily, soon, in our days.

Etz Haim/Hashiveinu – Return Us

Linda Friedman

עֵץ חַיִּים הִיא לַמַּחֲזִיקִים בָּהּ, וְתֹמְכֶיהָ מְאֻשָּׁר. דְּרָכֶיהָ דַרְכֵי נֹעַם, וְכָל נְתִיבוֹתֶיהָ שָׁלוֹם. הֲשִׁיבֵנוּ יְיָ, אֵלֶיךָ וְנָשׁוּבָה, חַדֵּשׁ יָמֵינוּ כְּקֶדֶם.

I am grateful for this "tree of life" that God has given us to follow its "ways of pleasantness" and "its paths of peace" and "renewal." It is my privilege to participate in Torah study classes to incorporate these goals into my life.

Etz Haim/Hashiveinu – Return Us

Jill W.

If you would have told me twenty years ago that I would be sitting here, writing a submission for a book about Jewish prayers, I would have thought you had mistaken me for someone else. Perhaps you were thinking I was an observant Jew or someone who had at least attended religious school as a child.

Certainly you wouldn't be thinking of someone like me who grew up in a secular Jewish household and, after being raped at age 17, spent most of her adult life questioning the existence of God.

I will never forget sitting at Yom Kippur services just a few weeks after enduring the worst experience of my life. I sat there reading how God protects those who obey his commands and punishes those who don't. My eyes filled with tears as I wondered why God didn't protect me and what I had done to deserve this. I wondered if God even existed and if he did, why anyone would want to believe in a God that would either intentionally cause or blindly allow something like this to happen. My attendance at that service marked the end of my participation in organized Judaism for many years.

Flash forward about 15 years. I am now married and have two children. My husband wants to join a congregation so our children can attend religious school. He comes from a family of Holocaust survivors.

How could I refuse? We enrolled my daughter in religious school and my son in our congregation's preschool. To avoid feeling hypocritical, I took adult education classes and occasionally even attended services. I tried to believe what my children were being taught, but whenever I attended services, all of the feelings I had on that awful Yom Kippur would resurface.

Despite my feelings about the liturgy and doubts about the existence of God, I did maintain a strong emotional connection to some cultural traditions and to *one single* prayer that I would hear on our occasional visits to synagogue on Saturday mornings. Whenever the members of our congregation would chant the last three lines of the prayer that is recited after the *Sefer Torah* is returned to the Ark, I would feel a strange chill throughout my body. I had no idea what the verses meant. They felt simultaneously somber, yet strangely uplifting, and always left me feeling an undeniable connection to the people chanting beside me. These few verses had the uncanny ability to make me feel connected to Judaism – even though I had just begrudgingly sat through an entire service reading things I simply did not believe.

One day, while this prayer was being chanted, instead of looking at the transliteration, I read the translation. It was quite telling. The verses seemed to be about returning to God. Returning to Judaism. Finding peace. Without even knowing the meaning, it was as if that prayer had been beckoning me to return to my roots.

After several conversations with our open-minded Rabbi and a very supportive adult education teacher, I eventually came to understand that prayers in the *siddur* do not have to be taken literally, so I began to reconsider the liturgy that made me turn away from Judaism so many years ago. I began to see God's admonitions to obey his commands or suffer the consequences in a totally different light. Perhaps the readings that once troubled me were actually intended to express the idea that if you live your life in a manner consistent with God's attributes, including those of compassion and the ability to forgive those who have harmed you, you will be able to flourish and live in peace despite the circumstances surrounding you. On the other hand, if you spend your entire life being angry, bitter and resentful, you will never be at peace and will likely suffer throughout all of your days. At that point, I realized that whatever God was or wasn't, it was within my own power to regain the spiritual peace that I believed God truly represented.

While the last three lines of a single prayer beckoned me to return to Judaism for many years, it was not until I learned a new way to interpret the other prayers in the *siddur* that I was finally able to once again feel comfortable attending Jewish services.

To this day, those three verses continue to send a chill throughout my body whenever I hear them. It's a good chill and reminds me that, despite everything I have been through, I somehow managed to return. I have found peace within myself, within a Jewish community and even while attending religious services. While I still struggle with my personal conception of God, I no longer see this as an obstacle to my participation in Jewish prayer services.

After nearly two decades of feeling estranged, I have finally returned home.

> *Etz hayim hi lamahazikim bah, v'tomkhehah m'ushar. D'rakhehah darkhei no-am, v'khol n'tivotehah shalom. Hashiveinu Adonai elekha v'nashuvah, hadesh yameinu k'kedem.*

It is a tree of life for those who grasp it, and all who uphold it are blessed. Its ways are pleasant, and all its paths are peace. Help us turn to You, Adonai, and we shall return. Renew our lives as in days of old.

Chapter 8
Closing Prayers

A good workout requires both a warmup and a cooldown. So, too, with prayer. Even though weekday prayers are often said rather quickly, because people have to get to work and school, we take the time to wrap our prayers in some closing words.

On Shabbat as well, a series of codas have been added over time to the service to enable us to gradually depart from prayer.

— *Rabbi Steven A. Schwarzman*

Ashrei

Herb Daroff

אַשְׁרֵי יוֹשְׁבֵי בֵיתֶךָ, עוֹד יְהַלְלוּךָ סֶּלָה: אַשְׁרֵי הָעָם שֶׁכָּכָה לוֹ, אַשְׁרֵי
הָעָם שֶׁיְיָ אֱלֹהָיו: תְּהִלָּה לְדָוִד, אֲרוֹמִמְךָ אֱלוֹהַי הַמֶּלֶךְ, וַאֲבָרְכָה שִׁמְךָ
לְעוֹלָם וָעֶד: בְּכָל יוֹם אֲבָרְכֶךָ, וַאֲהַלְלָה שִׁמְךָ לְעוֹלָם וָעֶד: גָּדוֹל יְיָ
וּמְהֻלָּל מְאֹד, וְלִגְדֻלָּתוֹ אֵין חֵקֶר: דּוֹר לְדוֹר יְשַׁבַּח מַעֲשֶׂיךָ, וּגְבוּרֹתֶיךָ
יַגִּידוּ: הֲדַר כְּבוֹד הוֹדֶךָ, וְדִבְרֵי נִפְלְאֹתֶיךָ אָשִׂיחָה: וֶעֱזוּז נוֹרְאוֹתֶיךָ
יֹאמֵרוּ, וּגְדוּלָּתְךָ אֲסַפְּרֶנָּה: זֵכֶר רַב טוּבְךָ יַבִּיעוּ, וְצִדְקָתְךָ יְרַנֵּנוּ: חַנּוּן
וְרַחוּם יְיָ, אֶרֶךְ אַפַּיִם וּגְדָל חָסֶד: טוֹב יְיָ לַכֹּל, וְרַחֲמָיו עַל כָּל מַעֲשָׂיו:
יוֹדוּךָ יְיָ כָּל מַעֲשֶׂיךָ, וַחֲסִידֶיךָ יְבָרְכוּכָה: כְּבוֹד מַלְכוּתְךָ יֹאמֵרוּ,
וּגְבוּרָתְךָ יְדַבֵּרוּ: לְהוֹדִיעַ לִבְנֵי הָאָדָם גְּבוּרֹתָיו, וּכְבוֹד הֲדַר מַלְכוּתוֹ:
מַלְכוּתְךָ מַלְכוּת כָּל עֹלָמִים, וּמֶמְשַׁלְתְּךָ בְּכָל דֹּר וָדֹר: סוֹמֵךְ יְיָ לְכָל
הַנֹּפְלִים, וְזוֹקֵף לְכָל הַכְּפוּפִים: עֵינֵי כֹל אֵלֶיךָ יְשַׂבֵּרוּ, וְאַתָּה נוֹתֵן לָהֶם
אֶת אָכְלָם בְּעִתּוֹ: פּוֹתֵחַ אֶת יָדֶךָ, וּמַשְׂבִּיעַ לְכָל חַי רָצוֹן: צַדִּיק יְיָ בְּכָל
דְּרָכָיו, וְחָסִיד בְּכָל מַעֲשָׂיו: קָרוֹב יְיָ לְכָל קֹרְאָיו, לְכֹל אֲשֶׁר יִקְרָאֻהוּ
בֶאֱמֶת: רְצוֹן יְרֵאָיו יַעֲשֶׂה, וְאֶת שַׁוְעָתָם יִשְׁמַע וְיוֹשִׁיעֵם: שׁוֹמֵר יְיָ אֶת
כָּל אֹהֲבָיו, וְאֵת כָּל הָרְשָׁעִים יַשְׁמִיד: תְּהִלַּת יְיָ יְדַבֶּר פִּי, וִיבָרֵךְ כָּל
בָּשָׂר שֵׁם קָדְשׁוֹ, לְעוֹלָם וָעֶד: וַאֲנַחְנוּ נְבָרֵךְ יָהּ, מֵעַתָּה וְעַד עוֹלָם,
הַלְלוּיָהּ:

Though I have led Shabbat morning services for over thirty years, I have to rely on the *siddur's* translation to understand what I have chanted in Hebrew. Though the *Ashrei* appears twice on Shabbat morning, during *Birkhot Hashahar* and at the end of the Torah service, the translations in our *siddur* differ dramatically:

The earlier translation is declarative:

> *He fulfills the desire of those who revere Him; He hears their cry and delivers them.*
>
> *All who love the Lord He preserves, but all the wicked He destroys.*

The later translation is aspirational:

May God always hear the prayer of the pious, always answer their pleas, come to their aid.

May God guard every loving soul, and destroy all wickedness.

I am more drawn to the aspirational. We are praying to God and hoping that He will fulfill our desires. And I envision God praying to us and hoping that we, too, will fulfill His desires that we behave as we perceive God behaves toward us.

Aleinu

Rabbi Steven A. Schwarzman

עָלֵינוּ לְשַׁבֵּחַ לַאֲדוֹן הַכֹּל, לָתֵת גְּדֻלָּה לְיוֹצֵר בְּרֵאשִׁית, שֶׁלֹּא עָשָׂנוּ כְּגוֹיֵי הָאֲרָצוֹת, וְלֹא שָׂמָנוּ כְּמִשְׁפְּחוֹת הָאֲדָמָה, שֶׁלֹּא שָׂם חֶלְקֵנוּ כָּהֶם, וְגֹרָלֵנוּ כְּכָל הֲמוֹנָם (שֶׁהֵם מִשְׁתַּחֲוִים לְהֶבֶל וָרִיק וּמִתְפַּלְּלִים אֶל אֵל לֹא יוֹשִׁיעַ) וַאֲנַחְנוּ כּוֹרְעִים וּמִשְׁתַּחֲוִים וּמוֹדִים, לִפְנֵי מֶלֶךְ, מַלְכֵי הַמְּלָכִים, הַקָּדוֹשׁ בָּרוּךְ הוּא. שֶׁהוּא נוֹטֶה שָׁמַיִם וְיֹסֵד אָרֶץ, וּמוֹשַׁב יְקָרוֹ בַּשָּׁמַיִם מִמַּעַל, וּשְׁכִינַת עֻזּוֹ בְּגָבְהֵי מְרוֹמִים, הוּא אֱלֹהֵינוּ אֵין עוֹד. אֱמֶת מַלְכֵּנוּ אֶפֶס זוּלָתוֹ, כַּכָּתוּב בְּתוֹרָתוֹ: וְיָדַעְתָּ הַיּוֹם וַהֲשֵׁבֹתָ אֶל לְבָבֶךָ, כִּי יְיָ הוּא הָאֱלֹהִים בַּשָּׁמַיִם מִמַּעַל, וְעַל הָאָרֶץ מִתָּחַת, אֵין עוֹד:

עַל כֵּן נְקַוֶּה לְךָ יְיָ אֱלֹהֵינוּ, לִרְאוֹת מְהֵרָה בְּתִפְאֶרֶת עֻזֶּךָ, לְהַעֲבִיר גִּלּוּלִים מִן הָאָרֶץ וְהָאֱלִילִים כָּרוֹת יִכָּרֵתוּן. לְתַקֵּן עוֹלָם בְּמַלְכוּת שַׁדַּי, וְכָל בְּנֵי בָשָׂר יִקְרְאוּ בִשְׁמֶךָ. לְהַפְנוֹת אֵלֶיךָ כָּל רִשְׁעֵי אָרֶץ. יַכִּירוּ וְיֵדְעוּ כָּל יוֹשְׁבֵי תֵבֵל, כִּי לְךָ תִּכְרַע כָּל בֶּרֶךְ, תִּשָּׁבַע כָּל לָשׁוֹן: לְפָנֶיךָ יְיָ אֱלֹהֵינוּ יִכְרְעוּ וְיִפֹּלוּ. וְלִכְבוֹד שִׁמְךָ יְקָר יִתֵּנוּ. וִיקַבְּלוּ כֻלָּם אֶת עוֹל מַלְכוּתֶךָ. וְתִמְלֹךְ עֲלֵיהֶם מְהֵרָה לְעוֹלָם וָעֶד. כִּי הַמַּלְכוּת שֶׁלְּךָ הִיא, וּלְעוֹלְמֵי עַד תִּמְלוֹךְ בְּכָבוֹד: כַּכָּתוּב בְּתוֹרָתֶךָ, יְיָ יִמְלֹךְ לְעוֹלָם וָעֶד: וְנֶאֱמַר, וְהָיָה יְיָ לְמֶלֶךְ עַל כָּל הָאָרֶץ, בַּיּוֹם הַהוּא יִהְיֶה יְיָ אֶחָד, וּשְׁמוֹ אֶחָד:

Judaism is a success. Never mind the latest demographic studies. Never mind anti-Semitism. Never mind hatred of Israel. Judaism introduced monotheism to the world, and the spread of this idea to roughly half of the world's population can only be called a smashing success. From Zion, Torah has indeed gone out.

That said, there is still some theological work to do. And this prayer reminds us of this fact. It's our duty – *aleinu* – to praise the Lord of all, the one who created the universe and the same one who made our small people, the Jews, not like all the other peoples of the world. And if you look closely at the Hebrew text, it is *because* God did not make us like all the nations, or our lot like theirs, that it is our duty to thank God.

Much of Western culture – a culture far removed from the Eastern culture in which this prayer was first written – is homogenizing. The power of the shopping mall and advertising and social media combine to make everyone want to fit in and to demand that they fit in.

And Judaism says, "no, thank you." You can have that stuff if you want, but while we, too like nice things, material goods and pop culture don't define who we are. What defines us is our distinctive worship of the One God, the Holy One, the Ruler of all.

Which is why the second paragraph of *Aleinu* is not a universalistic prayer at all, unlike what some *siddurim* say. It is a fervent hope that, one day, the other peoples of the earth will also recognize the One God, casting aside the various non-gods they worship now. It is a plea that they will accept God's rule – kingship in the Hebrew text – and that God will begin ruling over them, just as God rules over us, speedily and forever.

In an age of conformity, we do not conform, and it is our duty, sometimes, to insist on being who we are and not conforming.

Mourner's Kaddish

Rabbi Steven A. Schwarzman

יִתְגַּדַּל וְיִתְקַדַּשׁ שְׁמֵהּ רַבָּא. בְּעָלְמָא דִּי בְרָא כִרְעוּתֵהּ, וְיַמְלִיךְ מַלְכוּתֵהּ
בְּחַיֵּיכוֹן וּבְיוֹמֵיכוֹן וּבְחַיֵּי דְכָל בֵּית יִשְׂרָאֵל. בַּעֲגָלָא וּבִזְמַן קָרִיב וְאִמְרוּ
אָמֵן :

יְהֵא שְׁמֵהּ רַבָּא מְבָרַךְ לְעָלַם וּלְעָלְמֵי עָלְמַיָּא :

יִתְבָּרַךְ וְיִשְׁתַּבַּח, וְיִתְפָּאַר וְיִתְרוֹמַם וְיִתְנַשֵּׂא וְיִתְהַדָּר וְיִתְעַלֶּה וְיִתְהַלָּל
שְׁמֵהּ דְּקֻדְשָׁא בְּרִיךְ הוּא לְעֵלָּא (בעשי״ת וּלְעֵלָּא מִכָּל) מִן כָּל בִּרְכָתָא
וְשִׁירָתָא, תֻּשְׁבְּחָתָא וְנֶחֱמָתָא, דַּאֲמִירָן בְּעָלְמָא, וְאִמְרוּ אָמֵן :

יְהֵא שְׁלָמָא רַבָּא מִן שְׁמַיָּא וְחַיִּים עָלֵינוּ וְעַל כָּל יִשְׂרָאֵל, וְאִמְרוּ אָמֵן :

עֹשֶׂה שָׁלוֹם בִּמְרוֹמָיו הוּא יַעֲשֶׂה שָׁלוֹם עָלֵינוּ וְעַל כָּל יִשְׂרָאֵל, וְאִמְרוּ
אָמֵן :

Now and then, people who can't come to a *minyan* ask me or tell me about saying *Kaddish* on their own.

I understand why they want to do this. *Kaddish,* they know, is about honoring the memory of their loved one, and if they can't say it in *shul,* they figure they can say it at home. Maybe even better than in *shul,* in a quiet and comfortable environment.

But *Kaddish* is not a mourner's prayer at all. Not in the least.

It began with a *midrash* that a child leading the prayer service, eliciting the responses from the congregation to *Barkhu,* to *Kedushah,* and to *Kaddish,* could elevate the soul of a deceased parent.

Over time, it became apparent that not all Jews could lead the prayer service. So the last *Kaddish* of the service – which needed to be said anyway, not because it had anything to do with mourners or mourning – began to be reserved for a mourner to lead. It wasn't the same thing as leading the entire service, but at least the mourner would lead the service for a moment or two, and elicit the congregation's response: *Amen, yehei shmei rabbah mevorakh l'alam ulalmei almaya* – may God's great name be blessed forever and ever.

And, over time, instead of only one person being chosen to lead that *Kaddish*, based on the prescribed system of priorities (for example, someone with a *yahrzeit*, which is only one day, would trump someone in their year of mourning), all mourners began to recite *Kaddish* together, and the congregation would answer *amen* to all of them.

So far, so good. It's a little tricky, in terms of *halakhah*, for all these people to be leading the service at the same time, but this practice is now very widespread, and for good reason, because now all mourners can honor their loved ones' memories.

With this understanding of what saying *Kaddish* is about – eliciting the response of the congregation – it becomes clear that saying *Kaddish* without a *minyan* of pray-ers loses that call to the public that elicits the response of a holy congregation. It really is about that response.

And what is the response actually responding to?

To understand this, we need to understand that just about every printed *siddur* gets the text of the *Kaddish* wrong in a small but very significant way.

My teacher, Rabbi Miles Cohen, taught me that the eighth word in the *Kaddish* is given the wrong vocalization in most *siddurim*: where it says כִרְעוּתֵהּ - *khirutei* – it should say *kirutei*. If you know Hebrew, the difference is the *dagesh*. If there is one, it means that the word is separate in meaning from the one before it. If there isn't, it means that it's connected with the word before it.

Your eyes may be glazing over from what looks like a grammar lesson, but it's a cosmic point. In the way we print it in most *siddurim*, here is what we are saying:

> May God's great name be magnified and sanctified in the world that he created *the way he wanted to*.

Contrast this with the correct version:

> May God's great name be magnified and sanctified in the world that he created, *as is his will*.

The world as we know it is imperfect. We feel this imperfection more acutely when we are mourning. The usual spelling makes it sound like this is the world that God felt like creating, and if we don't like it, tough for us.

The correct spelling is completely different. It recognizes that this world needs improvement. The world needs God's great name to be magnified and sanctified, because *that is God's plan, and it has been since Creation.*

So when we pray the *Kaddish*, we do it publicly, in a *minyan*, because we can't fix the world all by ourselves. We express the call – and the congregation responds. *Amen, may God's great name be blessed forever and ever.* May God's redemption come speedily in our days. And, as Dr. David de Sola Pool wrote, a *minyan* of *shul*-goers who pray together and learn Torah together are a natural first step.

It's not *Kaddish* that elevates the souls of our loved ones. It's praying and learning with a *minyan*. And calling to the other pray-ers to join in praying and working for God's world to be perfected is a perfectly good way to elevate the souls of our loved ones – and our own souls, too.

Mourner's Kaddish

Adriane Gilder

Kaddish is my favorite prayer. I have six each year. When I go to the cemetery, I do a seventh. I don't just recite the Mourner's *Kaddish*, but I take the time to remember. I start each year with my father, Julius "Doc" Gilder. His *yahrzeit* comes at the end of April. I like to take the time to remember things, like long before GPS was available. If I had to go somewhere, he would hold the directions given to me by the hostess. I would drive my old beat-up 1962 Pontiac Tempest, and we would make a dry run to wherever I needed to go. That was when gas was 19 cents a gallon. He would mark each turn with landmarks to remind me to "turn left at the green house with white fence" or "turn right at the corner of "Stub Toe and Burnt Finger," then pray that the owners would not change the property.

Every Sunday on Labor Day weekend, we would go to the cemeteries. We would start out heading to Sharon Memorial Park to visit his parents, Esther and Harry Gilder, my paternal grandparents. From there, we would go to Woburn for my maternal grandparents, Fannie and Harry Brick, stopping at this nice pastry shop where my parents would order coffee and share a blueberry muffin. I got orange juice and a cranberry muffin. After Woburn, we headed to Everett for my great-grandparents' graves, Rabbi Samuel Hirshberg and Rebbetzin Celia Hirshberg. Then I would drive home. My mother got to relax in the back seat and my father would ride in the front, guiding me through the roads. Each light that was green for him was now red for me. He would engage a big belly laugh as no matter where and when I drove, I got every red light. He called me his red light princess.

Early May is my paternal grandmother. I like to remember her with our fun times of cooking and baking for all of the holidays. There was a photo of me and her. I'm sitting on a chair at about the age of 3. I have a towel wrapped and tied around me for safety. She has given me a wooden bowl, a spoon and a little bit of dough. And with her Yiddish accent, she would tell me to stir. By the time I was about 8, I could make the best *challah*, *mandel* bread, *tzimis*, *gefilte* fish, *kreplach*, chopped liver, and every other holiday food known to (Jewish) mankind.

In July, I take a few moments to once again say *Kaddish*. This is for my maternal grandmother, Fannie, *aka* Devorah. Sadly, she had a massive stroke four years before I was born. Her mind and body were severely impaired. Occasionally, when we would visit, she would be able to be reminded who I was. I remember how once her mind was clear. She hid her medication in a tissue, telling all of us that her pills made her crazy. I remember the day my mother took out one of my favorite dresses. It was blue and zipped up the front. She said that we were going to Boston to visit my grandmother. Since her functions had deteriorated more, this dress would be easy for the nurses to dress and undress her. My mother expected a revolt. Instead, I was overjoyed that one of my favorite dresses would go to her. It was so pretty with her olive complexion and very dark brown eyes.

In September, I say *Kaddish* for my paternal grandfather. I like to take the time to remember his loving arms and how he teased me because of my not very Jewish nose. Once he went through a red light while driving in his big orange Desoto, the one with a rectangle steering wheel and pushbutton transmission, and was stopped by the police. I was very young. When the officer asked him for his license and registration, I began an award-winning tantrum, screaming "Don't arrest my granddad!" I was crying like there was no tomorrow. The officer returned my grandfather's license to him along with the registration, telling him to be careful. Within a block, I stopped crying. My grandparents laughed at my Oscar-worthy performance. My grandfather, red-faced, said he would always remember that and, shortly before he died, he did. While I sat next to his hospital bed, he *kvelled* to the nurses, telling them all about how I saved him from a huge traffic violation. I can even giggle at it today.

In October, it's time to remember my Zadie, my maternal grandfather. I recite my *Kaddish*. I remember how he taught me to sew; he was a tailor, and did not fully retire until the age of 82. For years, we played cards and Po-ke-no. I remember a day when I was about 15. All of a sudden, his big robin's egg blue eyes opened wide and I got "the look." He motioned for me to sit beside him. "Asnah Kailah, it's snowing down south." He meant that my slip was showing. He continued, "Your birth certificate says your name is Adriane Karen Gilder. But don't forget you have Brick blood in your veins. Don't make a shame for the neighbors."

Finally, in December, *Kaddish* is for my mother, Ruth. I recite my *Kaddish* once again. I like to take the time to remember several of our adventures. Every Wednesday, when my father had late office hours, she and I would go out for supper, during which we would discuss how all short people should get together and overthrow the government. Tall men just couldn't get anything right. And I remember one morning she phoned me, insisting that I come to get her. We were going to her favorite mall, to spend every cent my father had made for the last six months and for the next six years. When I got to the house, there were four huge holes in the living room wall. Seems the curtain rod had broken and my father had tried to fix it. Right! Now, my father could pull apart every piece of his optometric equipment, clean it, and put it back together twice a year. He would then cover it for the time between Rosh Hashanah and Yom Kippur and for Passover, when he never did any shop work. When it came to the house, however, the man couldn't change a light bulb without calling a master electrician. We went to Filenes, where the first things my mother bought were new socks, t-shirts, and underwear for my father. Then she and I got several pairs of high heels and stylish dresses and went for a fabulous lunch.

When I go to Sharon Memorial Park, I do a seventh *Kaddish*. It's for my father's younger brother, Morton "Jack" Gilder. In 1965, my aunt died. About a year later, Uncle Jack called my father at his office asking him, my mother, and me to come to their home in Brookline so that I could have "the talk" with my cousin, Ronni. I started to explain the facts of life. Ronni began to laugh. She said her friend's mother had told her all the things she needed to know. But we didn't tell our parents that. While saying *yahrzeit Kaddish* for my uncle is the responsibility of my cousins, I feel like it's my *mitzvah* to say a *Kaddish* for him before *Yontiff*.

So *Kaddish*, yes, *Kaddish* is my prayer to honor.

Mourner's Kaddish

Joanne Gray

One of the upsides of saying *Kaddish* for a loved one is the people that you meet on your journey and what you learn from them. When I was saying *Kaddish* in 2001 for my Dad, Charles Goldbloom, a lovely gentleman, Wilf Levin, was saying *Kaddish* for his Mom.

Wilf suggested to me that, once I had memorized the *Kaddish*, I recite it with my eyes closed and visualize my Dad, as he was doing for his Mom.

It was *so* comforting to see my Dad. I usually visualized him with my late brother, Stephen, playing cards or gardening; he appeared happy and relaxed. On my last day of saying *Kaddish* for him, I had an odd sensation. I didn't see him above me, but felt him resting on my shoulder. I interpreted this as my knowing that he would always be with me.

Saying *Kaddish* for my Mom, this year, has been another spiritual and emotional ride. I look forward to "seeing" her. Sometimes she "appears" in her younger days; sometimes she's the older version. At times, she's wearing a housecoat; other times, she's in a party dress. She's often with my Dad; sometimes they are dancing, and she's often with Stephen. I feel happiest when I see the three of them together, yet at the same time it's bittersweet – a reminder of how much I've lost.

I'm not always successful at "tuning in" to her, during my prayers, but when I do, I feel comforted and stronger.

Thank you, Wilf, for this tremendous gift.

Shir Hakavod – Anim Zemirot (Shabbat)

Linda Friedman

These are the phrases in this prayer that hold the deepest meaning for me, because they speak to my personal feelings for God:

> *That while Thy glory is upon my tongue,*
> *My inmost heart with love of Thee is wrung.*

> *I glorify Him, for He joys in me,*
> *My crown of beauty He shall ever be!*

> *His glory is on me, and mine on Him,*
> *And when I call He is not far or dim.*

And lastly, I fervently pray:

> *Do thou receive it with acceptant nod,*
> *My choicest incense offered to my God.*

> *And let my meditation grateful be,*
> *For all my being is athirst for Thee.*

The Psalm for Sunday – Psalm 24

Rabbi Steven A. Schwarzman

לְדָוִד מִזְמוֹר, לַייָ הָאָרֶץ וּמְלוֹאָהּ, תֵּבֵל וְיֹשְׁבֵי בָהּ: כִּי הוּא עַל יַמִּים יְסָדָהּ, וְעַל נְהָרוֹת יְכוֹנְנֶהָ: מִי יַעֲלֶה בְהַר יְיָ, וּמִי יָקוּם בִּמְקוֹם קָדְשׁוֹ: נְקִי כַפַּיִם וּבַר לֵבָב, אֲשֶׁר לֹא נָשָׂא לַשָּׁוְא נַפְשִׁי, וְלֹא נִשְׁבַּע לְמִרְמָה: יִשָּׂא בְרָכָה מֵאֵת יְיָ, וּצְדָקָה מֵאֱלֹהֵי יִשְׁעוֹ: זֶה דוֹר דּוֹרְשָׁיו, מְבַקְשֵׁי פָנֶיךָ יַעֲקֹב סֶלָה: שְׂאוּ שְׁעָרִים רָאשֵׁיכֶם, וְהִנָּשְׂאוּ פִּתְחֵי עוֹלָם, וְיָבוֹא מֶלֶךְ הַכָּבוֹד: מִי זֶה מֶלֶךְ הַכָּבוֹד, יְיָ עִזּוּז וְגִבּוֹר יְיָ גִּבּוֹר מִלְחָמָה: שְׂאוּ שְׁעָרִים רָאשֵׁיכֶם, וּשְׂאוּ פִּתְחֵי עוֹלָם, וְיָבֹא מֶלֶךְ הַכָּבוֹד: מִי הוּא זֶה מֶלֶךְ הַכָּבוֹד, יְיָ צְבָאוֹת, הוּא מֶלֶךְ הַכָּבוֹד סֶלָה:

My paternal grandfather, Morris Schwarzman of blessed memory, was still working as an attorney at age 90. He shared an office on a service road next to a busy highway. One day, I visited him at work, and we were walking along the sidewalk of the service road on our way to lunch.

A woman was having car trouble, and asked us if we were able to help. But the issue was beyond the simple mechanical knowledge that he or I had, so he politely apologized to her. And then he did something that I remember every time that I have recited this psalm ever since, which is every time that the Torah is returned to the ark on a weekday or Shabbat afternoon service, and also on Sundays, when it is read in the morning service as the psalm of the day.

My grandfather made a joke that the woman couldn't possibly have understood. But I did. He said that we would have helped if we were able, and that the reason we couldn't wasn't because we didn't want to get our hands dirty, because we had clean hands. Or something to that effect.

He was referring to this psalm, I'm sure. *Who shall ascend the mountain of the Lord? And who shall rise up in God's sanctuary? One who has clean hands and a pure heart...*

He wanted her to know, though there was no way she could understand, that he had clean hands and a pure heart, and that if he could, he would have been happy to get his hands dirty to help her fix her car. And, I'm quite sure, he wanted me to know as well, not just that his hands were clean and his heart pure, but to teach me to keep my hands morally clean and my heart pure.

A wonderful lesson from my grandfather, one that gets repeated every week. Thank you, Pop-Pop!

The Psalm for Wednesday – Psalms 94 and 95:1-3

Heshy Rosenwasser

הַיּוֹם יוֹם רְבִיעִי בַּשַּׁבָּת שֶׁבּוֹ הָיוּ הַלְוִיִּם אוֹמְרִים בְּבֵית הַמִּקְדָּשׁ:

אֵל נְקָמוֹת יְיָ, אֵל נְקָמוֹת הוֹפִיעַ: הִנָּשֵׂא שֹׁפֵט הָאָרֶץ, הָשֵׁב גְּמוּל עַל גֵּאִים: עַד מָתַי רְשָׁעִים יְיָ, עַד מָתַי רְשָׁעִים יַעֲלֹזוּ: יַבִּיעוּ יְדַבְּרוּ עָתָק, יִתְאַמְּרוּ כָּל פֹּעֲלֵי אָוֶן: עַמְּךָ יְיָ יְדַכְּאוּ, וְנַחֲלָתְךָ יְעַנּוּ: אַלְמָנָה וְגֵר יַהֲרֹגוּ, וִיתוֹמִים יְרַצֵּחוּ: וַיֹּאמְרוּ לֹא יִרְאֶה יָּהּ, וְלֹא יָבִין אֱלֹהֵי יַעֲקֹב: בִּינוּ בֹּעֲרִים בָּעָם וּכְסִילִים מָתַי תַּשְׂכִּילוּ: הֲנֹטַע אֹזֶן הֲלֹא יִשְׁמָע, אִם יֹצֵר עַיִן הֲלֹא יַבִּיט: הֲיֹסֵר גּוֹיִם הֲלֹא יוֹכִיחַ, הַמְלַמֵּד אָדָם דָּעַת: יְיָ יֹדֵעַ מַחְשְׁבוֹת אָדָם כִּי הֵמָּה הָבֶל: אַשְׁרֵי הַגֶּבֶר אֲשֶׁר תְּיַסְּרֶנּוּ יָּהּ, וּמִתּוֹרָתְךָ תְלַמְּדֶנּוּ: לְהַשְׁקִיט לוֹ מִימֵי רָע עַד יִכָּרֶה לָרָשָׁע שָׁחַת: כִּי לֹא יִטֹּשׁ יְיָ עַמּוֹ, וְנַחֲלָתוֹ לֹא יַעֲזֹב: כִּי עַד צֶדֶק יָשׁוּב מִשְׁפָּט, וְאַחֲרָיו כָּל יִשְׁרֵי לֵב: מִי יָקוּם לִי עִם מְרֵעִים, מִי יִתְיַצֵּב לִי עִם פֹּעֲלֵי אָוֶן: לוּלֵי יְיָ עֶזְרָתָה לִּי, כִּמְעַט שָׁכְנָה דוּמָה נַפְשִׁי: אִם אָמַרְתִּי מָטָה רַגְלִי, חַסְדְּךָ יְיָ יִסְעָדֵנִי: בְּרֹב שַׂרְעַפַּי בְּקִרְבִּי, תַּנְחוּמֶיךָ יְשַׁעַשְׁעוּ נַפְשִׁי: הַיְחָבְרְךָ כִּסֵּא הַוּוֹת, יֹצֵר עָמָל עֲלֵי חֹק: יָגוֹדּוּ עַל נֶפֶשׁ צַדִּיק, וְדָם נָקִי יַרְשִׁיעוּ: וַיְהִי יְיָ לִי לְמִשְׂגָּב, וֵאלֹהַי לְצוּר מַחְסִי: וַיָּשֶׁב עֲלֵיהֶם אֶת אוֹנָם וּבְרָעָתָם יַצְמִיתֵם, יַצְמִיתֵם יְיָ אֱלֹהֵינוּ: לְכוּ נְרַנְּנָה לַיְיָ, נָרִיעָה לְצוּר יִשְׁעֵנוּ: נְקַדְּמָה פָנָיו בְּתוֹדָה, בִּזְמִרוֹת נָרִיעַ לוֹ: כִּי אֵל גָּדוֹל יְיָ, וּמֶלֶךְ גָּדוֹל עַל כָּל אֱלֹהִים:

The civil year 2004 was a terrible time in Israel. There was a horrible plague of suicide/homicide bombings in places like the Mahaneh Yehudah market and various buses in Jerusalem, to name but a few. I was living in Los Angeles at the time, geographically far away, but very much in tune with what was going on in our holy city and land. It affected me not only because of my part of the collective consciousness that unites all Jews, but also because of my personal history and connections there. I had spent many of my formative years in Israel, and my immediate family was and is all there. I knew the neighborhoods, streets, landmarks, and bus lines that were attacked. It felt like every attack on our beloved holy city was an attack on me.

What made it worse was how those perpetrating these monstrous attacks claimed to do so in the name of their deity ... supposedly the same deity that we Jews worship. After all, all monotheists worship the same One God, the Creator of the Universe ... do we not? How could this be? I had a very hard time squaring this with my spiritual perception of the world.

One Wednesday morning after a particularly gruesome attack, I found myself at a local *minyan*. As we edged toward the end of *Shaharit*, I recited that day's *Shir Shel Yom* (psalm of the day), which I must have mumbled many, many times since I learned about it in second grade. How many Jewish men speed through the song of the day with their impatience mounting, waiting for the instant when they can take their *tefillin* off, eat breakfast, and go to work? Most, I would speculate, and I was no different. But today, the words jumped right off the *siddur* page and demanded my attention.

> *Can the throne of destruction be associated with You?—those who fashion evil into a way of life. They join together against the soul of the righteous, and the blood of the innocent they condemn. (Psalm 94:20-21)*

King David's voice sings across the ages, rhetorically asking us now whether God is really with those who claim to be acting in His name. It was as if the Psalmist saw exactly what would take place millennia after his time, in the city he made his capital.

But then he offers hope, declaring what ultimately would happen to those who dare to kill us and have the unmitigated gall to claim that it was a divine command:

> *Then Hashem became a stronghold for me, and my God, the Rock of my refuge. He turned on them their own violence, and with their own evil He will cut them off, Hashem, our God, will cut them off. (Psalm 94:22-23)*

And when God finally turns the tables on the brazen murderers, it will be a time for rejoicing, akin to the happiness and contentment of Shabbos. For we will finally be able to rest, knowing that our enemies are no longer a danger to us. It is no mistake that the last three verses of the song for Wednesday are the same three verses that open the *Kabbalat Shabbat*:

> *Come, let us sing to Hashem, let us call out to the Rock of our salvation. Let us greet Him with thanksgiving, with praiseful songs let us call out to Him. For a great God is Hashem, and a great King above all heavenly powers. (Psalm 95:1-3)*

These words and this song became a touchstone for me, offering me comfort and strength whenever another dose of bad news would be broadcast from Israel. Could the throne of destruction really be associated with God? I would ask myself. The answer was then, and is always, a resounding NO. Our enemies may claim to be serving God, but their god is a false idol of destruction and child sacrifice—the ancient Canaanite cult of Molech transmogrified to the present day. We who worship the One God do not serve the same god that our enemies do. We should take heart from the words of our greatest earthly king, and may we see the imminent arrival of his descendant.

Chapter 9
Thoughts on Jewish Prayers

The *siddur*, the prayerbook, is actually a means, not an end. We sometimes forget that. Of course, the whole purpose of prayer is to connect with God. Sometimes the words printed on the page catapult us head-over-heels into a deeper connection than we ever imagined possible. And sometimes it is life itself that does this.

– *Rabbi Steven A. Schwarzman*

Prayer in My Life

Norman Stern

What a pleasure to think about prayer in my life. Praying has not been too easy for me in places of worship, but I find that praying without restriction to time and place is most satisfying. This gives me the ability to respond to a feeling at a random moment. Above all, what a wonderful experience it is to have a private conversation with God.

Actually, my initiation to prayer started many, many years ago. My parents suggested that I bless all my father's and all my mother's family when I go to bed. I felt guilty if I left out anyone. To this day, I remember how seriously I took this effort.

When I started school, we were required to say the Lord's Prayer each morning, along with pledging allegiance to the flag. This has a good effect for the start of the day – somewhat like the minyan.

Through the years, my mother wrote sayings from the Bible and suggested that I read them in times of stress and anxiety.

When I enlisted in the army at eighteen years old and before I left for Europe, my mother handed me the 91st Psalm to keep in my wallet. This started me enjoying many psalms, and now I enjoy my favorites like Psalms 91, 121, 23, 24, 103, and 139.

During the war in France and Germany, I read the psalms and the paper that my mother asked me to carry in my wallet. These prayers were very handy when I needed a crutch in war conditions. I find myself saying many of these phrases in my conversations with God.

The beauty of nature, with an active life near water, mountains, deserts, and woods, have aroused a gratitude in me and always have initiated a gratitude to God. Also, the meditations in the prayer books during the holidays and Sabbath have become familiar and add substance to my prayers.

The prayers in the Reform services I find very poetic and emotional – and very formal. But I especially enjoy the Conservative and Orthodox prayers, particularly the cadence intermingled with singing the traditional tunes, which are more spontaneous. Just listening at times supplies moments conducive to my praying.

When I am alone in a natural environment, I give thanks through my makeshift prayers. I occasionally talk to people who have died and were close friends – and I also talk with living close friends. After these conversations, I sometimes feel content and experience a warm feeling and an appreciation of this gift of life, and thank God for looking out for me and my wife and children.

I look forward to better understanding the prayers in the siddur.

The Year I Said Kaddish for my Father

© *Frances Kraft*

The year I said *Kaddish* for my father, I found myself transported back to my 1960s Hebrew school classroom, where my classmates and I had learned much of the prayerbook by rote.

In 2008, more than four decades later, page numbers from the slim blue siddur of my childhood would pop into my head unbidden, an amusing distraction from the meditative nature of the service.

Barukh She'amar… page 39! *Ashrei*… page 56!

I remembered the cadence and measured beat that went along with the words of some of the prayers, so rhythmic that we could have marched to it. Maybe we even did.

All these years later, at the end of the *Shma*, I still sometimes hear a distant echo in my head, the voice of my Grade 1 Hebrew school teacher finishing the prayer with us, and adding a word of instruction: "*Beitekha, u'visharekha, lashevet.*"

For years, it was hard for me to separate her authoritative last word – a directive to sit down – from the real end of the prayer.

I searched for my long unused Hebrew school prayerbook for a long time, and finally found it.

Siddur Shvil Chadash looked just the way I remembered it, with its dark blue cover and pale blue lettering on the outside; inside, shiny white pages and black, easy-to-read Hebrew letters. I turned to page 39, then 56 and a few others, validating my flashbacks one by one. My sister Karen shared the same vivid memories.

One day, Karen said to our mother, "You know how you always told me, 'One day you'll thank me for sending you to Hebrew school?' Well, I'm thanking you now!"

Our mom had waited a long time to hear that. She never imagined how much it would make us all laugh.

After my father died, and I began attending services regularly to say *Kaddish*, I discovered a new favorite prayer – *Tahanun*. It's not a popular prayer, and the reason I liked it had nothing to do with spirituality.

My father was a shul-goer, and many of the prayers in the *siddur* reminded me of him. Especially in the early days of the *Kaddish* year, when my emotions were close to the surface and my dad's voice still vivid in my head, the melody of familiar prayers threatened to evoke unwanted tears.

So I looked forward to *Tahanun*, a respite in the service because it was unfamiliar. A prayer with a pleasant tune that didn't remind me of my dad meant less chance of a grief attack. The nice melody was a bonus.

The *Shir Shel Yom* (Psalm of the Day) is recited at the end of the morning service, before the final *Mourner's Kaddish*. I discovered it – or perhaps rediscovered it – as an adult. I'd long forgotten, if I ever knew in the first place, that Shabbat was not the only day to have its own psalm.

But it wasn't the psalm per se that appealed to me during my *Kaddish* year. Rather, it was the single line in Hebrew written above each psalm, a reminder that the words were recited by the *Levi'im* (Levites) in the time of the Temple.

The introductory line was the best part, I thought. I wondered why it didn't appear in the English translation on the facing page.

Saying *Kaddish* connected me to generations past, but the Psalm of the Day – specifically, the line that precedes it – connected me to a time long before my known ancestors ever lived.

Sometimes it was the only thing on the page that I read.

Chapter 10
More Ordinary
Prayers

If you have thought of yourself as an ordinary pray-er, perhaps reading some thoughts from your fellow pray-ers gives you some ideas about how extraordinary Jewish prayer can be – and is, for people who also think of themselves as completely ordinary.

– *Rabbi Steven A. Schwarzman*

Ordinary Prayers are...Extraordinary

Rabbi Steven A. Schwarzman

Prayers are only ordinary if we allow them to be ordinary. "Ordinary" people can find extraordinary meaning in Jewish prayer. We, too can make our prayers extraordinary by letting them take us out of our routine enough so that we can savor the words, the sounds, the meanings, the associations that come to mind.

If you would like to share your own favorite prayer from the Jewish prayerbook, please write to me at ordinaryprayers@gmail.com – perhaps there can be another edition of this book with more "ordinary" prayers.

May each time you pray bring you some new, extraordinary sense of connection with God and with the Jewish people...and with the best parts of your own soul.

Let your voice be heard!

Chapter 11
Contributors

Rabbi Steven A. Schwarzman is a second-career rabbi, having previously worked as a writer for an Israeli software company and as a translator. He has served congregations in the United States and Canada, and loves helping Jews find their voices in deep Jewish prayer. This is his fourth book; he is the editor (with Rabbi Dov Peretz Elkins) of *Enveloped in Light: A Tallit Sourcebook*, in addition to two books on technical writing and training. He and his wife, Bettina are the parents of four children. He is the rabbi at Shaar Shalom Synagogue in Thornhill, Ontario.

Rabbi Rachel Barenblat was ordained by ALEPH: the Alliance for Jewish Renewal, as a rabbi in 2011 and as a *mashpi'ah ruhanit* (spiritual director) in 2012. She holds an MFA from the Bennington Writing Seminars and is author of three book-length collections of poetry: *70 faces: Torah poems* (Phoenicia Publishing, 2011), *Waiting to Unfold* (Phoenicia, 2013), and the forthcoming *Open My Lips* (Ben Yehuda Press, 2015), as well as several poetry chapbooks. Her free / downloadable *Velveteen Rabbi's Haggadah for Pesach* has been used around the world. A 2012 Rabbis

Without Borders Fellow, she has blogged as The Velveteen Rabbi since 2003; in 2008, TIME named her blog one of the top 25 sites on the internet. She serves Congregation Beth Israel, a small Reform-affiliated congregation in western Massachusetts, where she lives with her husband Ethan Zuckerman and their son.

Barry Barnes is a Conservative Jew active in the leadership of Shaar Shalom Synagogue in Thornhill, Ontario, and has spent his working career in both the private sector and in public service.

Rabbi Samuel Barth was appointed Senior Lecturer in Liturgy and Worship at The Jewish Theological Seminary in the summer of 2011. He was ordained at Leo Baeck College in London, following undergraduate studies in Mathematical Physics and Philosophy at the University of Sussex and the Open University (UK). He is completing doctoral work at New York Theological Seminary, exploring the use of Psalms in the interfaith context. Recently, he served as a congregational rabbi in Austin, Texas, and Gloucester, Massachusetts. In the past, he served as dean and senior vice president for Academic Affairs at the Academy for Jewish Religion, a pluralistic seminary in Riverdale, New York, where he was instrumental in establishing the cantorial program and a second campus in Los Angeles. At an earlier stage in his career, he was assistant dean of The Rabbinical School of The Jewish Theological Seminary. In his current position at JTS, he developed *Living Liturgy*, a new course for first-year rabbinical and cantorial students that approaches liturgy through many lenses – the literature of *halakhah* and *minhag*, the history of the *siddur*, and also through ritual theory and performance studies.

Rabbi Jack Bloom, Ph.D. is a rabbi and clinical psychologist, and one of a handful of rabbis who are full members of both The Central Conference of American Rabbis (Reform), and The Rabbinical Assembly (Conservative). He has become known as a rabbi's rabbi. In addition to his private practice at The Psychotherapy Center in Fairfield, Connecticut, he serves as Director of Professional Career Review for his Reform colleagues, for whom he created a program to assist rabbis seeking to shape their futures. Working closely with Conservative rabbis, he mentors and teaches regularly at the Rabbinic Training Institutes sponsored by his alma mater, The Jewish Theological Seminary of America. For ten years he was rabbi of Congregation Beth El, Fairfield, Connecticut, during which time he completed a STM in Pastoral Counseling from New York Theological Seminary. He earned a Ph.D. in Clinical Psychology from Columbia, and his dissertation, *The Pulpit Rabbi as Symbolic Exemplar* was the first of his extensive writings on what it's like to be a rabbi. He is the author of four books. He and his wife Ingrid, a gifted artist and retired German teacher, reside in Fairfield, Connecticut. They are the parents of four children and grandparents of seven.

Hazzan Shoshana Brown received her cantorial ordination from ALEPH: The Alliance for Jewish

Renewal in 2011 as the culmination of many years of study of Jewish texts, history, theology, music, liturgy, and practical work in the field as a cantor, music director, hospital chaplain, religious educator of children and adults, freelance writer and adjunct professor. She was raised in the Episcopal Church, and although she converted to Judaism at the age of 27, she believes that many positive church experiences have influenced her as a cantor, such as her enthusiasm for group Psalm-singing, both in English and in Hebrew. She graduated from Smith College in 1980 with a B.A. in English literature, but with a special interest in the relationship of poetry, philosophy, and prophecy. She has been a visiting graduate student at the Hebrew University in Jerusalem, and studied for a year at Machon Pardes. She holds an MPhil in Midrash from JTS. She has *davened* in every kind of congregation within Judaism, from Orthodox to Conservative to Reform, Reconstructionist, Renewal, and unaffiliated. She takes God, *mitzvot*, spirituality, *tefillah* (prayer), and social-eco-action (*tikkun olam*) seriously, while also believing that Judaism needs to be updated to meet the needs of the 21st century. She has benefitted enormously from her affiliation with Jewish Renewal, which she credits with adding joy, creativity, greater emotion, and elements of the mystical-hasidic path to her toolbox as a spiritual leader.

Cantor Jack Chomsky has served Congregation Tifereth Israel since 1982. He is Past President of the Cantors Assembly. He has written widely about prayer and spirituality in Judaism, and is active in interfaith programming, community organizing, and justice in his community and Israel.

Herb Daroff is an attorney by education and a financial planner by profession. He was a volunteer leader of Shabbat services and volunteer Sunday school teacher for over 30 years in Sharon, MA before moving to Worcester, MA last year. Herb's only formal Jewish education came from attending Hebrew School in Philadelphia, two days a week after school and on Sundays, and from active participation in Junior Congregation.

Edwin R. Frankel is a veteran Jewish educator and ritual specialist. He is equally comfortable with leading *tefillot* and the exploration of their content. He is convinced that the Jewish liturgy, even its most prosaic portions, must be considered as poetry, with subtle nuances and ever evolving meaning. Currently, he is the owner of Frankel Fine Foods, a home-based kosher caterer, and Thrive Jewishly, an agency for ritual and educational consulting. He is widely published on numerous educational themes. This is his first contribution to a book on Jewish prayer.

Linda Friedman was born in 1945 in New York City – a time when girls weren't necessarily offered a Hebrew School education. Orthodox grandparents gave her the foundation for a love of Judaism and tradition. Her spiritual journey developed as an adult over many years – giving her the faith in God to see her through personal losses and to be grateful for her blessings, motivating her to expand her Jewish knowledge through informal and formal classes, and providing her with a caring community in Toronto through her active involvement in her synagogue, first at Beth Emeth Bais Yehuda Synagogue and currently at Shaar Shalom Synagogue.

Joan Gaffin lives in Worcester, MA. Through all of her physical and emotional pain in her life experiences, she has learned to trust in the power of prayer. Deepening her faith in Judaism, she has learned to keep her heart open through the grief and stay connected in love and compassion.

Rabbi Lisa Gelber is the Associate Dean of the Rabbinical School, Rabbi of the Seminary Synagogue, and Adjunct Lecturer in the Department of Professional and Pastoral Skills at the Jewish Theological Seminary. She is also the project leader at JTS for the Tikkun Middot Project, a national program to explore inner attitudes and character development through mindfulness practice and refinement of moral qualities. A trained spiritual director, with certification from the Yedidya Center for Jewish Spiritual Direction, she incorporates intentional, compassionate listening into her work and everyday life. At JTS, she guides students as they reflect on what it means to become rabbis and engage in discernment about who they are becoming as spiritual leaders. She is a member of the JTS Committee on Gender and Sexuality, and helps to ensure the presence of co-curricular programming related to issues of gender and sexuality at JTS. She created and co-facilitates the Senior Women's Group for graduating students in the Rabbinical and

Cantorial schools. Editor of numerous works on domestic violence in the Jewish community, including *A Journey Towards Freedom: A Haggadah for Women Who Have Experienced Domestic Violence* (FaithTrust Institute, 2003), she served as a panelist on a parallel program of the 57th session of the UN Commission on the Status of Women (2013) and appeared in the interfaith documentary *I BELIEVE YOU: Faiths' Response to Intimate Partner Violence*. As the parent of a small child, she has a particular interest in the developing spiritual lives of children and the power of contemplative practice to deepen family relationships. A marathon runner for whom running serves as spiritual practice, she is a long-time supporter of the Leukemia and Lymphoma Society's Team in Training endurance sports program. A *magna cum laude* graduate of Amherst College, she earned an MA (1994) and Rabbinic Ordination (1996) from JTS. She served as rabbi of Herzl-Ner Tamid Conservative Congregation on Mercer Island, Washington and was the first rabbi of Congregation Kehillat Shalom in Skokie, Illinois. She was featured in the documentary *ALL OF THE ABOVE: Single, Clergy, Mother*, and lives in New York with her Torah muse – her daughter, Zahara.

Adriane Gilder grew up in Boston/Maynard, Massachusetts and has lived in Northborough since 1958. She has written a cookbook for those who benefit from local food pantries. The book, *Measuring Makes Me Itch*, contains 150 recipes where a minimum of half of the ingredients come from the food provided at the pantries. She was a C-Level Executive

Administrative Assistant for more than 30 years, and now as a semi-retiree contributes to her community by volunteering. She is a member of Congregation Beth Tikvah in Westborough, MA, where she bakes *challah* for every service.

Gayle Golden, LICSW, is a licensed independent clinical social worker with a bachelor's degree in Sociology from Smith College and a master's degree in social work from Simmons College School of Social Work. In addition to a private practice specializing in couples treatment and work with patients and families coping with chronic and terminal illness, she has been on the staff of the New England Medical Center and Massachusetts Eye and Ear Infirmary, providing direct patient care as well as training for medical residents and social service staff. She has been an adjunct professor in the Health Sciences Department at Worcester State University and Copace program at Clark University. She served as first vice president of the Massachusetts chapter of The National Association of Social Workers.

Erica S. Goldman-Brodie was born in England and raised in Australia. She came to America as a teenager. She has a BA from Stern College for Women of Yeshiva University and an MS from Hunter College. She taught children in elementary inner-city schools for 37 years, until Stage Four endometrial carcinoma forced her to retire. Her articles include "Owing a Debt of Gratitude" in the Holocaust section of *Chicken Soup for the Jewish Soul* and "Claire-ing" in *Bridges Magazine*, Spring 2014 (published by Memorial

Sloan Kettering Cancer Center). She lives in Riverdale, NY with her husband, Rabbi Joseph A. Brodie.

Amy D. Goldstein has worked more than 20 years for the Jewish community in various organizations. Born in Detroit, she grew up with a deep appreciation of Jewish history, Zionism and activism. After graduating from the University of Michigan, she pursued a Ph.D. at the Jewish Theological Seminary – specializing in the cultural history of medieval Sephardic Jews. Subsequently, Amy used her knowledge of Christianity, Judaism, and Islam and her training as a cultural historian to help formulate policy, communicate, and train grassroots activists in the United States and around the world, representing the Jewish People and organizations in national and international agencies. She has also served as the liaison from the Jewish community to the Greek Orthodox Archdiocese of America for several years, and continues to consult government officials, faith leaders, and organizations about Judaism, the Jewish community, Israel, and other issues. Living in Houston with her daughter since December 2005, Amy currently works to improve the lives of low-income students.

Joanne Gray lectures in York University's Administrative Studies Faculty and has worked as Executive Director for many not-for-profit organizations.

Stephen Griffiths has just retired from a 47-year career as a military pilot and flying instructor with the Royal Air Force. He is a member of the Kol Nefesh Masorti Community based in Edgware in North London, and is also the founder and leader of the Lincoln Independent Jewish Minyan in Lincoln, some 140 miles north of London. He is a trained *shaliah tzibbur* focusing on Shabbat and High Holydays services. He is also very active in interfaith work with the Council of Christians and Jews and visits many schools and church groups in the local area to teach about Judaism.

Frances Kraft is a freelance writer and former staff reporter for *The Canadian Jewish News*. She blogs regularly about writing, about moving on after being downsized, and about food and chocolate, at franceskraft.wordpress.com. She is working on a book about the year she lost her father.

Keith Manaker lives in Orono, Maine. He has a 13-year-old son and a 16-year-old daughter. He is part of a small but active and involved Jewish community. He has served in leadership roles within his congregation for the past 10 years.

Judy Petsonk is the author of *Taking Judaism Personally: Creating a Meaningful Spiritual Life*, and the co-author, with Jim Remsen, of *The Intermarriage Handbook: A Guide for Jews and Christians*. Her novel, *Queen of the Jews*, was published in 2012.

Rabbi Perry Raphael Rank is the spiritual leader of Midway Jewish Center in Syosset, Long Island. He was ordained by the Jewish Theological Seminary in 1981. He is co-editor of *Moreh Derekh*, the rabbi's manual for Conservative rabbis, and past president of the International Rabbinical Assembly. He presently chairs the Long Island Rabbinic Advisory Council for UJA Federation of New York.

Rabbi Peretz Rodman is an American-born, Jerusalem-based rabbi and educator who has served Jewish communities large and small across the globe. He has taught at every level from elementary schools to graduate schools and theological seminaries (Jewish and Christian), published dozens of articles in journals, newspapers, and websites, and translated numerous works in Jewish studies.

Heshy Rosenwasser is a musician, writer, and editor whose journey through life reads something like the travelogue of his ancient Israelite ancestors through the desert. Beginning in suburban Long Island, he has also lived in Jerusalem, Asbury Park, Boston, Philadelphia, and Los Angeles, before landing in his current domicile in northern New Jersey, where he lives with his wife Cheryl. He has attended yeshiva (both high school and beyond), served in the Israel Defense Forces, and worked for Steven Spielberg's Shoah Foundation. He has belonged to numerous synagogues, but his favorite one by far is the Happy Minyan, Los Angeles' Carlebach congregation. He is currently in the process of recording his next CD and writing his first novel when he is not at his day job as an editor for a pharmaceutical advertising agency.

David Sefton is a Canadian Engineer, born in England during the Second World War. He is married to Marlene, and they have two boys and five grandchildren. Theirs is a mixed marriage of Conservative and Orthodox Jewry, although in the 1960s, unlike today, the difference between the two streams was minor. They were founding members of Shaar Shalom Synagogue in 1974. He has been active in Toronto Jewish communal activities since the early 1970s, and was the President of the Toronto Hebrew Free Loan Cassa (G'millas Chasadim) in the 1990s.

Bettina Schwarzman grew up in Sweden, lived in Israel, and now resides in Toronto. She enjoys leading services at her synagogue, and is a teacher of Hebrew language, Bibles, and synagogue skills including Torah and Haftarah chanting for children and adults. Her Jewish tutoring website is www.jewtor.com.

Norman Stern served in the US Army in World War II, has been a director of a Jewish summer camp, and is an active member of Congregation Beth Israel in Bangor, Maine, where he paints, teaches, volunteers for multiple charities, and studies Talmud at age 90.

Heather G. Stoltz is a fiber artist whose quilted wall hangings and fabric sculptures are inspired by social justice issues and Jewish texts. Stoltz, named as one of The Jewish Week's "36 Under 36" for 2012, received a 2011 Manhattan Community Art Funds grant for *Temporary Shelter,* her installation piece about homeless New Yorkers. Her work has been exhibited nationally and featured in *Jewish Threads, Creative Quilting: The Journal Quilt Project* and several other publications. She was a Drisha Arts Fellow 2008-2010 and was an Artist-in-Residence at the 2008 National Havurah Committee Summer Institute. Heather lives in Harrison, NY with her husband Geoffrey Mitelman and their daughter Caroline. Her work can be viewed at www.sewingstories.com.

Mark Wallach was born in Israel, moved to Canada at the age of 3, and has lived in the suburbs of Toronto most of his life. He has been practicing opticianry for 25 years and has been married to his wife and best friend, Natalie for 27 years. They have two sons: Daniel, soon to be certified as a social service worker specializing in geriatric care, and David, currently working towards his Masters in Jewish Education with their daughter-in-law Erin in Jerusalem.

Made in the USA
Middletown, DE
13 March 2015